Elite Dangerous - The Unofficial Handbook
Part 1: Beginners

www.ed-howto.com

Copyright © 2019 Alex M. Adams

Alex M. Adams
c/o Autorenservices.de
Birkenallee 24
36037 Fulda
Germany
grtfm@web.de

Print by Amazon Media EU S.à r.l.
5 Rue Plaetis
L-2338, Luxembourg

All rights reserved

ISBN: 9781098739478

Imprint: Independently published

Bibliographic information published by the Deutsche Nationalbibliothek

The Deutsche Nationalbibliothek lists this publication in the Deutsche Nationalbibliografie; detailed bibliographic data are available on the Internet at http://dnb.dnb.de

Index

1. About This Book..9
2. Ten Important Informations For A Good Start..11
    2.1. The Basic Structure Of The Elite World 12
        2.1.1 Travelling..12
        2.1.2 The Structure Of The Elite World.....................................13
        2.1.3 The Structure Of The Elite World - Global Powers............15
    2.2 Rebuy..18
    2.3. Fuel Scoop [module]..20
    2.4. The Power Distributor [module]..24
    2.5. The Eight Seconds Rule...26
    2.6. Ward Off Attacks..27
    2.7. Docking the right way...32
    2.8. Bad neighborhood...37
    2.9. Expensive Is Not Always Good..40
    2.10. Much Bigger Than You Think...41
    2.11. What I Wouldn't Do Today - Don'ts 42
    2.12. What I would advise a "newbie" – Dos......................................45
    2.13. A Brief Introduction To Missions..49
        2.13.1. The Docking Computer..49
        2.13.2. Pick Up Cargo, But Correct..51
        2.13.3 Horizons: Jump range...52
        2.13.4 Horizons: Materials...52
        2.13.5. The "instances" Thing..53
3. First Flight: An Example..55
    3.1 In The Station...55
    3.2 Departure...57
    3.3 Navigation And Jumping Into The Neighboring System..................60
    3.4 Navigation To The Station..62
    3.5 Approach And Landing...67
    3.6 At The Destination...70
4. Navigation..81
    4.1 Jump Range And Equipment..82

    4.2 Longer Distances 84
        4.2.1 The Galactic Map.. 84
        4.2.2 The System Map.. 88
        4.2.3 The Planet Map.. 89
        4.2.4 Neutron Stars... 89
    4.3 Nitromethane Injection [horizons]... 90

5. Income And What To Do Best For Beginners.. 91
    5.1 Ranks, Ranks, Ranks... 92
        5.1.1 The "Elite" Ranks... 93
        5.1.2 The Military Ranks... 97
    5.2 Missions... 99
        5.2.1 Introduction to the World of Missions... 100
    5.3 Combat And Survival.. 105
        5.3.1 Survival.. 106
        5.3.2 Combat.. 110
        5.3.3. Earning Money: Bounty Hunting... 120
        5.3.4 Law And Order In Elite Dangerous.. 125
    5.4 Exploration... 129
        5.4.1 Path To Wealth [HOWTO].. 131
        5.4.2 Real Exploration.. 136
    5.5 Mining... 137
        5.5.1 Basic Mining With A Very Small Ship... 139
        5.5.2 Advanced Mining With A Decent Income....................................... 142
        5.5.3 Deep Core Mining... 147
    5.6 Collecting Cargo In Space.. 151
    5.7 Wealth For The Impatient... 153

6. Ships – Shipyard And Outfitting... 156
    6.1 Buying Ships But Buying Them Right 157
    6.2 Modules.. 159
        6.2.1 Internal Modules / Compulsory Modules 162
        6.2.2 Optional Modules.. 174
        6.2.3 Utility modules.. 206
    6.3 Weapons.. 216
        6.3.1 The Damage Model 217
        6.3.2. Target Acquisition.. 220
        6.3.3 Types of weapons... 222
        6.3.4 Module Damage.. 237
        6.3.5 Engineers.. 238
        6.3.6 When it gets dangerous.. 243
        6.3.7 Miscellaneous... 244

7. External Information..245
    7.1 Finding things...246
    7.2 Building Ships..248
    7.3 News, Information and Space Selfies..............................249
    7.4 Addons..251
8. Connect To People..255
    8.1 Making Friends...256
    8.2 The Squadrons..257
    8.3 Discord...259
9. Hardware: Keyboard, Mouse, HOTAS.......................................260
10. Outlook..263
11. Annex: Road To Riches – The List 264

This book is NOT an official product for the computer game Elite Dangerous. This book has NO business relation to Frontier Developments.

Information in this book is publicly available and may include errors, I do not guarantee or assume any liability for any damages arising from its use, whether physical, mental or even virtual.

Elite © 1984 David Braben & Ian Bell
Frontier © 1993 David Braben
Frontier: First Encounters © 1995 David Braben
Elite: Dangerous © 2012, 2013 Frontier Developments PLC

All rights on all Elite versions are naturally with the authors, as well as the rights of all other marks in connection with Elite.
The pictures used in the book originate from the author himself and are subject to his copyright. Not from the author originating pictures are from Pixabay.de and are subject to the copyright noted there.

Passing on, copy, screenshots or other duplication (also partly) only with permission of the author.

1. About This Book

In here you will find everything you need to know as a beginner and moderately advanced 'commander' in the Elite Dangerous Universe.

From 'You better stick this to your screen with a post-it' tips to real basics for successful navigation, exploration, action, combat, equipping ships, to some tricks that make life easier. There's a lot to discover.

You won't find topics covered by the free in-game tutorials, nor will this book handle information you can get for free on multiple websites on the internet. If you are looking for the 'Fast Money Guide', have a look around Youtube, there are a lot of these videos.

Elite is so much more than 'to the Anaconda in one week', though!

It's the joy of growing and flourishing, of playing solo or in company, of making friends or playing in a group of like-minded players.

In other words, this book is what makes the difference between slowly finding out the most important things you need to know for Elite Dangerous and a carefree time with plenty of progress and one 'AHA' moment after another.

This book is aimed at beginners and slightly advanced commanders (and sometimes even for some 'professional', who might find something useful in it in spite of all of his or her experience).

Of course, it can't cover everything that happens in Elite Dangerous, but it can cover everything you need to know in the first hours, days and weeks of Elite to be a successful commander.

The structure may seem arbitrary to you at first, but it has a functional structure:

First of all, you will be confronted - on a few pages - with all the "Had I known this before" things which so often cause frustrations and rage quits, in case you are one of the "Yes, now I want to play first" representatives.

Afterward, there is a factual introduction to the first flight. You certainly have that one already behind you out of sheer curiosity, but you will still make these flights so often that it makes sense to show you all the subtleties to "make yourself comfortable and save time and effort".

The navigation chapter then shows you how you can safely reach distant destinations.

Then comes the chapter on money. Like today, this is also a core topic in the 34th century.

Afterward, you will learn everything that takes the frustration out of the topic "Ship purchase and equipment".

Finally, there are tips for external information gathering and for the "social" life around Elite.

The "Horizons" package can unfortunately not be dealt with here: Planetary landings, material collection, scrap collection, improving ships with the engineers, new ship types, weapon improvements and lots of other activities and options are the subject of another book that deals specifically with the tips and tricks needed in the Horizon package. So everyone can use the book they need

2. Ten Important Informations For A Good Start

Elite is - without any exaggeration - huge and absolutely overwhelming for beginners.

It is, therefore, all the more important to make a few things clear beforehand that can make the first hours of discovery a real hell if you don't pay attention to them.

The following ten tips are not ordered by importance, as you should have read and understood them all at least once to keep them in mind. So to speak the "right before left" and "right throttle, middle brake, left clutch" of the 4th millennium.

As the eleventh and twelfth points of this chapter, there's a collection of statements from experienced "commanders", by the way, what they would do differently or not if they started over. The dos and don'ts of the old stagers, so to speak.

2.1. The Basic Structure Of The Elite World

In the world of the elite, one must distinguish between the actual extent and the type of travel used momentarily.

2.1.1 Travelling

Traveling itself is explained easily, there are three-speed ranges:

2.1.1.1. Normal Speed

After undocking from stations (or after losing an enemy interdiction or winning one initiated by yourself), you are in regular speed range.

Velocity is given in meters per second (m/s). Ships in Elite are between approx. 150 and 450 m/s in regular speed. The Horizons expansion improves this using the Engineers: speeds up to 800 m/s and more are possible on some ships.

2.1.1.2. Supercruise

If you do not select a jump target outside the current system - i.e. either no target at all or a target inside the system – you will be moving around in so-called supercruise after charging your jumpdrive. Supercruise allows you to travel using speeds from km/s range up to several hundred times speed of light inside the current system! In this mode, speed needs some time to build up and is influenced by (planetary) mass a lot, so stay away from planets, rings and the like.

2.1.1.3. Hyperjump

By selecting another system ahead of activating the jump drive, you select hyperjump mode through „witch space" - infamous for Thargoids interdicting humans while jumping to another system (No worries, this only happens in „infested" systems.)

You can easily recognize another system by the „ly" (light years) marker behind its distance when using the navigational short list.

For a hyper jump to another system, you start by selecting a target. Then you charge your hyperdrive (FSD). When completely charged, you turn your ship to the destination using your compass (left of your radar screen) and accelerate your ship to full speed. If you got a high ship mass and weak thrusters you might need to boost once in order to align the ship's path with the path to your destination.

Arriving at the target system, you should immediately lower your thrust to 0% - standard key: „X" - for not going where your nose points at: the main star's hot close vicinity.

2.1.2 The Structure Of The Elite World

The detailed structure of the elite world cannot be completely dealt with in this chapter, its structure is too complex. Nevertheless, you should take time for the following short introduction. It will make things much easier for you in finding your way around.

2.1.2.1 The Galaxy

The Galaxy is based on our 21st-century data plus lots of additional systems inhabited - or found in the meantime. The result is a maximum of reality with a grain of SciFi.

2.1.2.2. The Bubble

The so-called „bubble" is the area of the galaxy that has been colonized starting from SOL. In this area, you will meet most of the other "commanders" (cmdrs). In addition, computer characters such as pirates, law enforcement officers, and others are also most frequently encountered here. Outside the bubble, there is another populated area called "Colonia", which is only 22.000 light years away... a (sarcastic) stone's throw away.

2.1.2.3 The Systems

Each system consists of a clear but highly individualized structure. Besides one or more main stars one finds (in the inhabited area) a beacon, planets, moons and all sorts of other interesting areas, signal sources and more.

2.1.2.4 The Planets

The planets are diverse. In the expansion package "Horizons" you can even partially land on them and drive on the surface. Partially, as this is only possible on planets without an atmosphere. Planets with an atmosphere are planned for updates in the next years (!).

2.1.2.5 The Stations

Like planets, stations can also be found in various designs, from the large agricultural station with habitat ring to the small (pirate) station in a hollowed out asteroid. All with different facilities from black markets to shipyards - in different "qualities".

Much more important than the detailed examination of this rough structure are the political structures that affect the entire course of the game.

2.1.3 The Structure Of The Elite World - Global Powers

The global powers are divided into three power blocs:
- The Federation
- The Empire
- The Independents.

Federation and Empire not only consider each other enemies, but they are also far from being of one opinion (even inside their power blocks) on a number of matters, so political issues are really complicated. Just like in real life.

The main figures of the Empire are members of the ruling family, in the Federation two more or less moderate and more or less elected politicians, in the Independents a motley bunch of powerful men from the utopian to the businessman.

The systems, in turn, are exploited or controlled by the main characters on the global level (so-called powerplay), but populated by so-called minor factions on the actual local level.

These minor factions are either groups that are computer generated or groups that are registered and supported by player groups.

Most of these player-supported groups have the same name as the player group.

However, there are exceptions, namely when a group of players has decided to "adopt" a small faction and work with it without it being immediately apparent from the outside that there is a connection between the computer-generated grouping and the group of players.

In other words, this is the special case of a computer faction that is more or less secretly supported by players. This is popular with smaller groups because you offer less "attack surface" compared to other player groups. With some groups, this is not part of the roleplay, but also and above all part of the behavior of the group.

Stations and planetary bases in the system are controlled by the minor factions. Depending on whether you as a player - no matter if you are a member of a faction or not - do good to this station or harm it, be it through trade, combat, missions or donations, you can influence the "influence" of the station to a not inconsiderable extent.

Computer characters are usually attached to one of the small factions. Doing evil for them - or catching a criminal from this group - also has an influence on the political situation. The same applies to other (criminal) activities.

Players can declare themselves as followers of one of the main characters or be members of a squadron.

At first glance, this overview may seem very complicated and - even worse - chaotic. In fact, however, it is a well-thought-out construct that allows players to participate in what is happening - even politically - but does not force them to play a particular role.

Unfortunately, the complexity of this BGS (BackGroundSimulator) would cause several hundred extra pages of explanation which is way out of scope for a beginners' manual).

Many "commanders" choose a role in the Elite universe that is not limited to a particular small faction, the main character, or global power. In fact, the strict representatives of a political line are in the minority, the most frequent being "commanders" who enjoy working with the so-called background simulator (BGS), i.e. influencing the political conditions in the systems in a targeted manner in the sense of a conviction or for a small fraction.

Elite is not a fixed one-layer-game in the classical sense, but according to your personal preference: What you make of it!

Consider it a giant playground or simulator, not an MMO or some quest based game. It does have features of several game genres, but the amount of personal freedom is way out of the scope of classical games.

2.2 Rebuy

In the not so unlikely event that your ship is shot off under your butt, or you lose your ship due to an operating error or carelessness, there is compulsory insurance in the elite world. This insurance replaces the whole ship together with armament and modifications (unfortunately no freight), under one condition:

You have got enough "free" money to pay the deductible in case of damage.

The deductible normally amounts to 5% of the replacement value and is called „rebuy". With a ship worth ca. 10 million credits you need about 500,000 credits in available „free cash".

The current value of the deductible/rebuy can be found inside your ship:

View to the right (default to access this view is "4" key) > Status > Bottom left > BALANCE (greater than REBUY COST)

It is important that you really have this excess at your disposal. If smaller ships fail, it may be possible to compensate some or all of the costs by means of a loan (the loan is deducted over time from the income earned thereafter), but for larger ships or sums this loan is not sufficient and the disaster occurs:

Your own ship cannot be replaced and you lose the equivalent of its worth by not getting it back in any way. No compensation. None.

This loss can be more than 300 million credits (e.g. Python) and up to 1.5 billion credits (e.g. Imperial Cutter) for larger ships.

Over the years I have experienced several "commanders" who had to return from larger ships like the Anaconda or the Federal Corvette to smaller ships with a loss in the hundreds of millions. Now smaller ships are usually more fun to fly, but the lost amount of money and the lost opportunities in terms of passenger transport, freight transport and combat hurt. Writing about the frustration of these "commanders" is really hard for me due to a lack of suitable words.

Notice:

Rebuy is essential.

Check before undocking.

Without exception

2.3. Fuel Scoop [module]

Traveling in Elite Dangerous is neither particularly arduous nor particularly dangerous.

With one exception:

Fuel shortage!

All ships have enough fuel for several jumps so most ships can reach between 50 and 150 light years without additional tanks or other aids.

Especially smaller and lighter ships or those designed for a short distance and combat operations have alarmingly short total ranges due to very small fuel tanks.

It is therefore highly recommended to take a close look at the Galactic Map when planning your journey. As long as the line connecting the individual intermediate waypoints is drawn through, everything is fine. A dashed line says that you don't have enough fuel from that waypoint on.

> **Notice:**
>
> **The dashed line in the routing = Out of fuel!**

The wise "commander" installs a fuel scoop in every ship that is not used for short-range commuter traffic. This module (installed in the optional module bay of a ship) takes up very little space, does not add weight to the ship and allows free refueling from suitable main stars. (The star type is displayed among other things when initiating a jump into the next system - or even on the galactic map. Main stars have a star in the navigation short list as marking.)

Definition of "suitable" is quite simple: All stars of the categories KGB FOAM fill your ship's fuel tank in no time (depending on the fuel scoop's size and your ship's fuel tank).

Notice:

KGB FOAM (not sorted alphabetically), can easily be remembered using a weird image: A certain KGB agent in a bubble bath. Well? Once you've thought it...

In order to use a Fuel Scoop, please read the message when activating the jump drive and find out the type of the main star you are jumping to. (If you haven't noticed this yet, whenever you activate the jump drive, you'll get a short message what kind of star it is that you're about to jump to.)

After jumping slowly (!) touch the outskirts of the main star until your Fuel Scoop is automatically activated by proximity. Then you can slowly "cuddle" closer to the main star as long as you make sure that the temperature doesn't rise above 100%, with a maximum of 80% heat being best for no module damage at all.

If you should ever come too close to the main star and fall back into the normal speed range in an automatic emergency drop, please remain calm. Not much happens as long as you don't panic. Simply stop and wait until the blue curl for cooling the jump drive has disappeared.

During the waiting time please open the left ship window (default: key "1") and select anything in the "Navigation" area of the current system.

Then load the jump drive (default: key "J") and follow the escape vector (blue circle, the compass helps to find it, it must be centered and unfilled). DO NOT BOOST. After jumping into supercruise, keep on going full throttle until the temperature is decreasing due to the distance to the main star. The - minimal - heat damage that occurs is quickly repaired at the next station.

If you are stranded somewhere without fuel and the chance to fill your tanks, please make a note of your exact location:

- Which system?
- How far from the main star?
- Near any prominent point?

After that please leave the active part of Elite and go back to the main menu (for not consuming your last drops of fuel while waiting for help).

Open a browser of your choice and then visit

https://fuelrats.com

The "Fuel Rats" are one of the oldest groups in Elite Dangerous. They specialize in the rescue of stranded pilots which ran out of fuel. These specially trained and highly professional rescuers - whose main professions range from explorer to pirate - come to the rescue on request: Free of charge and lightning fast – with a canister (or several if needed) of fuel.

Hint: Visit the website at least once for the incredibly adorable fuel rat logo!

2.4. The Power Distributor [module]

Now for the - by far - most important module of the ship, the power distributor.

The power distributor ensures the precise and useful distribution of your ships' power generator's power (actually: the heat dissipation) within the ship.

It's a mandatory module in the core utility section that should always be installed in the largest size (number) and „best performance" quality (A). Among other things, the power distributor determines the duration between possible boosts and the possible fire duration. To put it in a nutshell, the speed at which the three "main types of energy" are charged and the size of the possible stores or „buckets".

The power distributor is represented in the instrument panel and must be used wisely (!). Just look to the right half of the dashboard, to the left of the fuel gauge, for three columns and abbreviations named SYS, ENG, WEP, and RST.

RST means RESET and has the down arrow key preset. Once pressed, it distributes the six "pips" (the filled points under the small bars) evenly over all three parts, i.e. 2 pips per part.

SYS means SYSTEM and has the Arrow to LEFT key preset. Each press of this key assigns one more "Pip" to Sys.

> **Very important:** 4-Pips-in-SYS provides ca. 250% shield strength compared to 0-Pips-in-SYS. Moreover, the shields are healing much faster!

> **Notice:**
>
> **Always and without exception set 4-Pips-in-SYS if you are not 100% safe.**

ENG means THRUSTERS (Engines) and has the arrow UP key preset. Each press of this key distributes one more "Pip" in ENG.

The more pips in ENG, the more agility for your ship in normal speed mode, more top speed and faster booster recharge.

WEP means WEAPONS and has the arrow-to-RIGHT key preset. Each press of this key distributes one more "Pip" in WEP.

The more pips in WEP, the longer the fire duration and the less drain in the WEP bucket (column above the pips) - a higher level in WEP causes less heat development when using the weapons.

This is rather unimportant at the beginning but becomes more and more important with increasing complexity and size of the ships used. Learning to pay attention to everything related to the power distributor and its bucket levels is needed to advance further in combat at a later stage.

In every battle, whether in a Sidewinder or a Federal Corvette, the operation of the power distributor, and thus both energy and heat management, must have absolute priority.

> **Notice:**
>
> **The power distributor is the decisive factor!**

2.5. The Eight Seconds Rule

This rule does not describe how long a sweet may have been lying on the floor of a spaceship until unsafe for consumption. In supercruise between planets, this rule describes the time at which one must act. But first from the beginning.

If you're flying in supercruise mode towards a target, you should do it at full throttle. By staying away from larger masses (planets) the cruising speed increases rapidly and you soon bridge distances that were initially displayed with a crazy duration needed to reach them in way less time than expected.

"Full throttle" without limits, however, has the disadvantage of you completely screwing up the approach to a target and rush past it with plenty of excess speed. The result is the "loop of shame" to reach your goal. Loss of face, loss of time, big laughter in local chat, scattering ashes on your head, all that stuff.

If you instead just wait for the moment when 00:08 is shown in the approach timer (8 seconds, you see where this is going...) and then reduce the throttle (and thus the speed) quickly to the smallest (lowest) "blue" area, you are in the optimal speed for the approach.

(Note: Actually it's about 6 seconds here, that's the threshold of reason... but the 8 seconds rule only costs a little more time and make things much less stressful. So if you are brave and in a hurry, you can try the 6 seconds.)

> **Notice:**
> Full throttle to 8 seconds on the timer
> Then smallest blue thrust setting for fastest travel without loops of shame

For the sake of completeness, however, it should be mentioned here that the "loop of shame" does not necessarily have to be one, it can also save your skin depending on the circumstances.

If you are pursued by a pirate – no matter if human or NPC - while in a non-defensible ship - you ideally keep the setting at "full throttle" and aim close, very close (!), near the target planet.

The target planet with its large mass then slows the ship down enormously and deprives the pirate of the possibilities to intercept because of the huge change in speed and the flight path involved (no interdiction near planets). Immediately after passing the planet, the thrust is changed to "lowest blue setting" and the reversal curve is initiated.

NPC pursuers are rarely able to intercept you (and your position) during this maneuver, making it great for smuggling or dangerous missions with NPC following you.

Human pursuers must recognize this maneuver as such at an early stage (at this point simply hope your opponent didn't buy this book) and fly a precise maneuver with a well-equipped and agile ship with a large interdiction module (range!) in order to be successful. Very few "bad guys" are mentally and technically equipped for such things.

2.6. Ward Off Attacks

You're not always able to stand up to an attacker. Be it that one crosses your way while you're in a defenseless freighter, be it by one's own status as an "outlaw" after an exhausting (and perhaps not quite so legal) mission.

If you are intercepted by an attacker in supercruise, you should first place the throttle lever in the middle of the blue area. In this area, the possibility of influencing the interception process is greatest for all ships.

Right after that, you take a look at who's knocking. Default: "H" key.

Now you can either decide to let it come down to an "interdiction duel", then you center the appearing target as good as you can.

Tip:

If it is difficult to "catch" an outwardly moving target, simply make changes to the thrust lever in very small steps. This requires some practice but is extremely helpful.

If you want to be sure not to be destroyed, or if you see that the red blocks are over 50% on the way up - and you run the risk of losing the interception process, it makes sense to submit to the interdiction. Default: Key "X" to set the thrust to 0%.

Thrust to 0% submits yourself to the pursuer, but creates, unlike a lost interdiction, some tremendous advantages:

No damage when entering the normal speed range
No wild tumbling around. Full capacity to act and no disorientation

No overheating of your jump drive. You can immediately concentrate on your escape.

After entering the normal speed range, everything must be done routinely and quickly to safely escape from a dangerous situation.

- Thrust into the blue area.

- Pull "Pips" in ENG (thrusters - see power distributor)

- Turn to the opponent, aim just to the side close to him.

- Boost to get behind the opponent (default: key "TAB")

- Boost a second time for maximum distance.

- Open left in-ship window (default: key "1"), select another system in the navigation area - recognizable by the abbreviation "ly" for light years

- Charge the jump drive, while continuing to boost straight ahead – don't fly curves, going straight ahead makes use of the smaller silhouette of most ships when seen from ahead or behind. Turning turns your silhouette into a huge target on most ships, especially the flat ones. Jump drive charging: (default: key "J")
- With the jump drive fully charged, turn towards the target without boosting (use the compass).
- After aligning to the target system, boost again to align the ship to the needed vector (in other words: boost so it doesn't drift anymore if you got a huge ship mass or weak thrusters). Key is the message shown „align with target system".

This procedure initially forces your opponent into a reversal turn. Your enemy's turn takes some time no matter if NPC or human and until this turn is completed, you have created lots of distance between yourself and your opponent at maximum speed.

Since all weapons lose their efficiency at a distance (called falloff point, e.g. regular lasers are losing damage against targets from about 500-600m of distance), the damage done is massively reduced. Straight boosts also prevent your own ship from showing its "big side" in any curves. (Most ships are shallow in shape and become a huge target in turns)

After jumping into the next system, you are safe from computer-generated opponents.

> **Caution!** Human "commanders" have the possibility to find out about your target system and follow you by estimating the jump direction (cycling all nearby systems after aligning with your direction) or by using scanners.

In the case of a human pursuer turn away from the main star after entering the target system while your FSD is cooling down (small blue symbol right below the fuel gauge).

After cooling down phase has ended, reduce speed into the km/s range and drop into normal speed range. (default: key "J")

In normal speed range, immediately open the left navigation window (default: key "1") and select another jump destination in another system.

Then charge the jump drive and jump to this system. Repeat this second jump in the next system one more time and you are also safe from pursuing players.

The background of this procedure is, that estimating the jump direction requires the pursuer to first align to your jump direction, then cycling through all potential jump targets.
To do so, he must see you in normal space to align with your direction – which is only possible in normal speed mode.
To see you in normal speed mode, he first has to find your „traces" - your „low wake" and follow this to the place you are in normal space.

In short: Your pursuer needs time to follow you he doesn't have. Game over – for him.
In a nutshell:
- Who's that?
- Fighting the interdiction
- Surrender
- 4-in-ENG
- Medium-blue thrust
- 2 x boost
- 1-NAV ? another system

- Load jump drive
- Fully charged? Align and...
- Boost for alignment

2.7. Docking the right way

Docking at stations is described in detail in the tutorials provided - one might think.

In real life, however, there is a multitude of smaller and larger tips and tricks (not: cheats) that make life easier.

Thus, the subsequent approach to the station can be made much easier by starting preparations for it in supercruise: Just consider that the (only) entrance to larger stations is generally roughly in the direction of the corresponding planet.

So it makes sense to fly to supercruise stations in such a way that at least in the last part of the supercruise approach your flight path originates from the planet.

How? Just aim for somewhere in between planet and station without getting to close to the planet (for not suffering from an emergency drop due to its vicinity).
When in between, turn toward the station. Observing the station's symbol on the left hologram, you can now fine tune your approach path if you like.

Once dropped and near the station, you should restrain your temperament by keeping your speed below 100 m/s.

Why that? Very simple: If you ram another ship at more than 100m/s and destroy it, the station will start an attack against you. Stations are big and they got an insane amount of firepower (and a weapon effect that will not only damage your ship it will snipe your shield generator to pieces in a second) On top of that there's a bounty on your head and a little vacation in the penal camp. Speeders are obviously not more popular in the 4th millennium than they are today.

By the way: Even if the other ship is not destroyed, a small fine will be imposed. Flying at sane speed helps.

If you have approached the station to 7,5km or less of a distance you have to apply for a landing permit. If this is omitted or forgotten and you still fly into the station, a timer starts, which gives you enough time to fly out of the station quickly and calmly. If you can do that in time, you get a little punishment, and that's all.

If you don't manage to leave the station within the given time because you panicked, the station will start shooting at you and we have already found out: you have to avoid stations which found a reason to open fire.

To apply for landing permission, proceed as follows:

- Open left window (default key "1")
- Press the "E" key to select the "Contacts" tab.
- Select the station (standard keys "W" and "S")
- Change to the right part of the window (standard key "D")
- Press button "Request landing clearance" (standard button "Space").

The fact that you really got the landing permission (now and then it doesn't work and you have to go through the procedure described above again) can be recognized by the fact that the number of the landing pad assigned to you appears in blue above the radar.

> **Notice:**
>
> **Landing permits are no joke at all.**

For smaller stations, capacity is limited, and queues often occur, especially in "open" game mode near social centers and active „community goal" destinations. Therefore, one should quickly finish one's work in the station and depart as soon as possible in order to free the landing pad. Using the hangar doesn't free the landing pad and many a "commander" was destroyed in a rage by other players when leaving smaller stations for blocking the landing pad for a longer time.

At larger stations capacity is not a problem due to the maximum number of ships per instance, but the approach is. Helpful for "Coriolis" stations - these are the dodecahedrons - the almost spheres with 12 outer surfaces - is an arrow display on the left "target" hologram of the dashboard after receiving landing clearance. Its arrows point to the entrance.

The approach itself should always be slow (see above - the holiday in the penal colony, you remember) and immediately after entering the station, the speed should be further reduced.

Please do not stop completely, especially directly after entering the „mail slot", otherwise "rear-end collisions" might ruin your day.

Finding the allocated landing area is then made easy once inside: Just use your compass left of the radar.

Notice:
COMPASS

Filled ball = Ahead of you
Empty ball = Behind you

If not being in a hurry due to being wanted or while smuggling goods, landing on the landing area should be done the same way no matter what type of ship and place to land - if there is enough time.

Place your ship above the landing pad in such a way that you face the displayed holographic landing numbers while still above the pad. If these numbers fill the windscreen, you are located above the landing surface and only have to lower the ship with slight corrections (move to the left with the standard key "Q", move to the right with standard key "E") with the vector thrusters. Use forward (standard key „W") or backward (standard key „S") thrust accordingly.

Your exact horizontal position on the landing pad can be seen on the radar screen. If both lines are blue from right to left as well as from top to bottom and the concentric circles are blue, you are directly above the bullseye. Just lower your ship now (default: key "F").

When touching down on the landing surface, the "rod" of the ship's symbol should be in the middle of the area shown in the radar field and the ship should be horizontal. The relative situation to the landing field is an important factor, especially for larger ships. Correct it using the mouse or your stick/controller.

A now rare but previously very annoying bug in Elite is that an NPC ship occupies the landing pad that was assigned to you.

Please do not try to land on this ship, do not try to shoot it or to displace it, this will fail and with a bit of bad luck get you killed.

Instead, you should fly out of the station, cancel the landing clearance, wait briefly, and then obtain another landing clearance.

Usually, a „really" free landing pad is assigned in 1-3 additional attempts.

If not: Go to the main menu (default: key "ESC") and switch to SOLO game mode. This respawns a new set of NPC and the error associated with coordinating players within an instance does not occur. (To a certain degree, this coordination is even present in SOLO mode, although players are invisible to you)

After you have landed in SOLO game mode you can switch back to open mode and continue playing. Remember: SOLO is OPEN without humans. Not more. Not less.

2.8. Bad neighborhood

Elite Dangerous includes a broad spectrum of different players from different backgrounds. From the "mature" older player, who already played the first 8-bit version in 1984, to the experienced power gamer of the latest generation. Elite manages to give the most diverse people a „future" home.

Unfortunately, however, a certain kind of person also finds a world in Elite in which they can really let off steam and feel mighty: People who enjoy destroying other players' enjoyment of their achievements and demonstrating their - supposed - superiority.

Of the really many participants in the Elite Universe, these are the very few, in fact only a few dozen, maximum a hundred. Fortunately, they almost always romp around in the same places, so that one can protect oneself quite well against them.

Unfortunately, it's the starter systems like LHS 3447, Eravate, Asellus Primus and LHS 3006 that are popular playgrounds for those who can't survive in real combat situations due to a lack of knowledge and skills and have therefore dedicated themselves to being serial killers on the defenseless.

They spend the day killing off fresh "commanders" in small ships and excuse this idiocy with arguments like "I show the developers that elite is a game not well designed" or "This is the salt in the soup of boredom".

Alternatively, these figures, who are clearly outside normal human behavior, repeatedly retreat into systems such as Wolf 397 or Deciat, where they attack "commanders" who fly into these systems in ships that are not ready for battle in order to have the "engineers" optimize their modules and weapons.

If the opportunity presents itself in the form of an active "community goal", these figures also fly there to distribute as much frustration as possible among the participants of these events in their "role".

It's important that these lines don't give the impression that Elite has the "spoil the game" proportions of some other games. It is also important to see that the vast majority of "commanders" in Elite - also and especially in comparison with other games and simulators - are very mature, friendly, helpful and polite.

Nevertheless, one should avoid these "bad neighborhoods".

If you are using the starter systems, engineer systems or systems with active community targets, please pay attention to hostile attackers who do not hesitate to destroy you without warning. Use private game groups or SOLO mode if you are traveling with cargo when losing it would kill to much progress or joy.

> **Notice:**
>
> **ALWAYS play it safe!**

2.9. Expensive Is Not Always Good

„Ships and their equipment" is a large and very complex part of Elite Dangerous.

Too many newcomers succumb to the misconception that larger ships are better and more expensive modules are more powerful. In the following you will see inexperienced "commanders" in ships for 300 million, 600 million or more than one billion (!) credits, who in their frustration to have lost just against a player with a ship costing only 10 million credits, give Elite Dangerous testimony of being an awful game.

This can be seen in all ship classes and also at the module level. Questions like "Why do I lose against a poorly equipped Cobra Mk3 when my ship only has the most expensive weapons and modules?"

The reason for this can be found in a special feature of Elite Dangerous:

Ships and modules have characteristics, not a pure performance that is bought with money.

In other words:
A well-built ship with an experienced "commander" can bring an average or poorly-built - much larger - ship with an average "commander" into distress or even destroy it.
If you keep a few basic rules in mind when building a ship and thus ensure a light but balanced setup, you can easily escape this danger.

These basic rules and the basic understanding of how to configure good ships for their intended purpose cannot be dealt with in this brief overview. Please read the chapter on equipping ships (chapter 6). It's worth it.

2.10. Much Bigger Than You Think

Elite is old. The first version of Elite was released in 1984.

Above all, however, elite is huge and completely unmanageable. At least at the beginning.

After some time, most of the "commanders" have an "I already know" effect, which leads to a kind of special arrogant boredom.

This effect can be quickly remedied if someone with more experience asks a question: "Have you ever made/seen/found XYZ?

In other words, the elite is what the inclined reader makes of it - with a myriad of options in terms of possible activities, roles, and goals.

Whether you're sailing through space, searching for alien worlds or fighting aliens, mining precious metals and defending yourself or others against pirates, helping stranded colleagues with a modern form of gasoline canister, fighting epic battles in highly modified ships, or simply flying a Cobra Mk 3 every now and then on a mission for your favorite political faction...

ELITE IS WHAT YOU MAKE OF IT!

2.11. What I Wouldn't Do Today - Don'ts

If you ask experienced "commanders" what instructions they would give their younger self to create a better time for you in the elite universe, you will always get the same answers:

Don't 1.) Start the "run" on the big ships

There's no way you're skipping ships. The big ships can do certain things that the smaller ones can't, but they're not always the better choice or generally "more fun". Sometimes even the opposite is the case. Rather buy all types of ships once, equip them once or even several times according to your personal preferences and simply have fun with the variety and "on the way up". Especially because Elite doesn't have an "endgame". Elite cannot be "played through", it is rather a kind of "second life in space".

Don't 2.) Grind

Do not allow yourself to enter "grind" mode. Many "commanders" are of the opinion that Elite is a "grind" game, one in which you have to do endlessly long repetitive (and boring) things to get ahead. Admittedly, you can get to certain ships, ranks or other financial destinations faster, but the fun must not be left behind. The danger of burning out from exhaustion or simply dying from boredom at the computer is too great.

Don't 3.) Consider ship "x" or "y" as bad

Elite has a number of ships that are rejected by a large number of players. Either because they are „too small" or „no fun", or because they simply don't like the ship's reputation. Examples for such ships are Cobra Mk4, Cutter, Type 7, Type 9 or the "federal dropship".

Understandable, because they are all in a way the "strange cousin" version of other ships, i.e. they are less fun to handle or like the Type 7, which – as an unmodded freighter - is certainly the most defenseless ship in the game, they simply "die" too fast. (Yes, I know there's also the Hauler, but it doesn't count. It dies even faster... but on a budget, it's a very cheap ship freighter.)

Only sometimes, or rather for some purposes, there is no way around these ships. The imperial cutter, for example, is simply the freighter par excellence and thus makes millions in bounties on the side, because it can not only run away but also really defend itself.

The same applies to all other types of these vessels. It just depends on what you do. A ship lives from your outfitting and you need to know what you want a ship to do for you when buying a new one.

Don't 4.) Use certain "professional" weapons

This refers mainly to beam lasers and cannons. I fully support this statement, because both are sub-optimal weapons at best without additional engineering only available in the Horizons package.

In the standard version, the beam lasers not only generate an enormous amount of heat but also suck so much energy from the power distributor that the "WEP" bucket is always empty when the laser is most urgently needed.

Cannons are neither hot nor energy-hungry but tend to miss just about anything more than 500 meters away, unless engineered with a long-range mod which gives them up to twice the projectile speed.

So: Both should be avoided unless the engineers can be called in.

By the way, this also applies to rail cannons, which are quite difficult to handle if you don't already have some experience with the rest of the flying in Elite. When not engineered a single one of these can ruin your heat management and make you cash in on heat damage in combat.

Although the plasma accelerators seem to be easier to handle, they have even more misfires than the cannons at longer distances because of their slow projectile speed. From the time you fire your weapon until the projectile reaches the target, a lot of time can pass – on an average distance of e.g. 1600 meters, there are almost two seconds in which your enemy can evade by constant motion. And he will.
In addition, both weapons are unreliable due to their huge power distributor energy consumption and overtax beginners mercilessly. That's just frustrating, so hands off first.

2.12. What I would advise a "newbie" – Dos

Just like the above "just don't" points, the "don'ts" there are also a number of "should you know" things called "dos".

Do 1.) Pay attention to „silent running"

If suddenly the blue shield rings on the left ship hologram are missing and "silent running" appears somewhere, then you have inadvertently initiated your own demise by pressing a button.

Shocked? Rightly so. "Silent running" deactivates your shields and is intended to make the ship less detectable (not completely invisible) to radar screens.

The problem: heat is no longer dissipated and your ship becomes warmer and warmer - until module failure occurs or your ship is destroyed.

If you have heat sinks on board, you can use them to bring the ship into a normal temperature range below 100% - or the range of less than 40% necessary to make silent running work in terms of less detection by enemies and stations.

Without a heat sink, you should immediately stop silent running mode (default: key "Del" via the arrow keys or the menu item in the right ship menu: Functions – silent running). Otherwise, this episode ends tragically.

Do 2.) Thinking about the insurance thing

The biggest frustration with newbies and also more experienced "commanders" is the loss of their own ship. Not the destruction and reappearance, but the complete loss - the step back from the 500 million ships into a nutshell for beginners. In the blink of an eye.

If the ship is destroyed - by an accident or an attack - you get an identical copy from the insurance if you have 5% of the purchase price for the ship including modules at hand.

> **Notice**: **ALWAYS check before departure:**
>
> **Right ship's window (default key "4") > Status, Bottom Left:**
>
> **More free money than rebuy!**
> **Loss of ship is a real concern if not!**

To a limited extent, missing rebuy money can be replaced (borrowed), but this only works up to relatively small sums. I can say from experience with dozens of "commanders": The loss of an Anaconda - e.g. worth 500 million credits - and the step back into a small ship is a terrible experience.

Like the Rolling Stones sang so beautifully "You make a grown man cry". The song is not about Elite, but the effect fits well.

Do 3.) Take a Fuel Scoop with you

Even spaceships need fuel, at least in Elite Dangerous.

Even ships with an above average total range like the Cobra Mk3 have only a limited amount of fuel on board. If this is used up, you can't jump any further at first, then systems fail and then... we don't want to paint black.

Whenever you plan more than one jump into a neighboring system, you should definitely take a Fuel Scoop with you. Even the smallest and cheapest Fuel Scoop in size 1E can refill your fuel tank after some time so that you don't get stranded or suffer ship destruction.

Usage is quite simple: After jumping into a system of the classes KGBFOA or M (main sequence stars), you simply fly a little closer - not too close - to the main star. The Fuel Scoop deploys and fills your tank. The closer you fly, the faster you refuel, but the more heat you generate. Rule of thumb: 80% heat. If it becomes more, create some distance to cool down.

The main sequence stars are quite easy to remember: KGB agent in a bubble bath.
Crazy? Yeah, sure – but that's why it's such a great reminder.

A former KGB officer in a foam bath is an image not easily forgotten. (Yes, I know: That's already in the book, but it's also so uber-important that you should emphasize it several times, just to be on the safe side, what I just did :-))

> ### Notice:
>
> **Scoopable stars: KGB FOAM**
>
> and
>
> **Fuel Scoop Rulz! (sic!)**

2.13. A Brief Introduction To Missions

The most important thing about missions is efficiency.

No matter if you are improving your reputation with a small faction (REP+), helping a small faction politically (INF+), or if you want to earn money, the more "plus" per time spent, the better.

With low ranks and low reputation with a faction, simple or urgent (boom time) data delivery missions or small cargo volumes are often the most effective way to reach your first goals. Read more in the mission section of this small manual, chapter 5.2.

2.13.1. The Docking Computer

Docking computers (better: flight assist modules) are double-edged swords.

As comfortable using this small optional module is, as negative are its potential side effects.

On the one hand, docking computers tend to create hair-raising situations at the worst possible moment: Failure due to an ongoing attack, unwanted scans, collisions, penalties or, in the worst case, a ship completely wedged into a station structure that can only be rescued with difficulty ... or not at all.

On the other hand, you become comfortable. So comfortable that you can no longer dock properly by hand over time. Worst case? Failed showboating on docking with spectators around. On a new, large ship. You might become a youtube star.

So please, only use the docking computer option when the time saved by it can be utilized in a better way, or when the boredom factor can no longer be surpassed, for example during long and repetitive freight missions.

You're lazy? Okay, here you go:

Standard Docking Computer – when near a station (below 7.5 km of distance), send a landing request. With this request accepted and active, place your throttle to zero and enjoy the show. Disrupt this module by advancing your throttle to more than 0%.

Advanced Docking Computer – same as above, but with an additional undocking function. When undocking... do nothing. As long as you don't touch anything, you will slowly be brought to a position roughly 5 km from your departing station. You can abort this module by simply advancing throttle to more than 0%.

Supercruise Assist – additional module that has to be activated. Select your target inside your system, just don't 'lock' it in your left navigation menu but use the button one to the right of your nav lock – supercruise assist. Then turn your ship to the target and place your throttle somewhere into the 'blue' range. Watch this module closely as your throttle will be at mid-blue after dropping, heading to the station...

2.13.2. Pick Up Cargo, But Correct

A not too small part of life in Elite's universe consists of collecting floating stuff in space.

When collecting flotsam manually, it is best to ignore everything you see "outside" and simply concentrate on centering the object to be collected in the small additional screen that appeared when the cargo scoop was extended.

If you keep the speed between 15 and 35 m/s and don't chase the object in case of a miss, but simply return to a calm starting position in reverse gear and try again, you've already gained a lot.

More helpful, however, is the information that there is a more convenient way to collect flotsam, namely the collector limpet controller. This optional module is available in different sizes (number of drones) and versions (range, the lifetime of drones).

Assigned to a fire key (default key: "4" fire groups) you can use these drones either to collect a single piece of flotsam by setting the flotsam to be collected as the target (default key: "T"). By doing so the limpet collects the object, then dies. Alternatively, you don't set a target when you launch the limpet. The limpet then collects everything it can see in its given range, then stays near the ship in standby mode. This "general" collection mode is usually preferable.

2.13.3 Horizons: Jump range

Many of the ships offered are not really of the long-range type.

If you are looking for a way to increase the range of these ships, Horizons „engineers" offer a way to significantly increase the FSD (Frame Shift Drive) range.

If you don't have access to an engineer yet, or if you have difficulties finding the required materials, you can install a Guardian Frame Shift Drive Booster. In size 5, this ancient high tech module offers over 10 ly more jump range, no matter how high the original range already is.

2.13.4 Horizons: Materials

Using Horizons' engineers you will experience a certain problem sooner or later: „I have tons of material A, but I need material B!"

For this, so-called material traders are used, which unfortunately are not available at every station. In general, refineries/extraction sites are most likely to find traders for element materials, high-tech sites are most likely to find data traders and industrial sites are most likely to find traders for prefabricated goods.
For information about the closest dealer near your current location, best use the very comfortable web page inara.cz - more on this in the corresponding chapter 7.3. Keep in mind that there are three different material traders for human stuff, none of these can swap materials not specified for their kind: raw, manufactured, encoded.

By the way: There are places with plenty of materials. These are dealt with extensively in the engineering part of the book series!

2.13.5. The "instances" Thing

Elite Dangerous has an in-game architecture that is rare for MMOs today: Instead of using single "game servers" or "nodes" there is no central server that acts as a node between the single "commanders".

Instead, Elite uses only a few servers, which on the one hand record the achieved performance (income, ships, launchings, movements), and on the other hand, generate a "matchmaking". All the rest of communication and coordination is done peer-to-peer, from Cmdr to Cmdr.

Thus, different "commanders" are paired according to factors such as "friend list", "similar behavior" and "similar strength". Of particular importance here is the geographical location of the players as in IP geolocation.

It is therefore rather rare to find "commanders" from other geographical regions in one's own "instance" (=one's own small world).
Only if you are active at times that are atypical for your own region, you may be assigned to the respective other geographical regions. All this because there are not enough other "commanders" of the same orientation available at 05:00 AM in the morning at your given location to create a complete instance.

If you don't see any other ships (unfilled radar symbols) in the starter systems despite your first successes in making money and (battle) rank, you should take a look at the suggestions given in the FAQ on IPv6, UPnP and Port Forwarding to find out how your network part can communicate properly with Elite.

At least at normal times, there should always be a few other ships around LHS 3447/Eravate after the first few hours of play, at least when you dock at one of the larger stations like Russell Ring. By the way, the instancing / matchmaking can also be influenced:

For example, you can set your status to "wanted" through minor crimes in order to see other "commanders" in your instance. Likewise one can find a completely different world by ship and weapon choice as matchmaking adapts to your behavior and ship setup in the game.

Where there were lots of nice people around you while in a benign freighter, in the sought-after Vulture all of a sudden everything is full of bounty hunters and other wanted people...

3. First Flight: An Example

This chapter is the actual introduction to Elite Dangerous. It is very helpful if you have already completed all the tutorials offered by the game. The previous experience of the tutorials is not absolutely necessary but very helpful, because this chapter describes mainly improvements to the tutorials, tips and tricks and small tricks, which are not immediately obvious at first sight.

3.1 In The Station

Since release, there were mainly two starter systems. 'LHS 3447' and 'Asellus Primus'. The former led most cmdrs to activities around 'Eravate', the latter around ... 'Asellus Primus'.

The last update brought a new 'safe space' for new elite players, a group of systems that is 'permit locked': only newbies can enter these systems until reaching their first higher rank.

As this beginner's manual can not see if you started at 'Dromi' inside this new safe space or if you started yet at LHS or Asellus, it will not waste too many pages for 'details': the procedure for the first flight is generally the same with mission destinations or targets-to-fly-to differing in name and – minimally – by structure.

In the end, Elite is a world-to-discover, so no worries, no matter where you fly to or what you do, your first flight will be a succeess. This chapter is mainly about undocking, simple navigation and docking at your destination. Hit the ground running!

LHS 3447 is a very large system with numerous stations, but they are all quite far away from each other. LHS 3447 is therefore not necessarily an example of a useful system. To understand what I mean, look at the system map after departure from the station but before jumping into another system, briefly! (Standard key "1") Travel times in LHS 3447 are ... impressive.

"Commanders" with horizons or other packages occasionally start in the system "Asellus Primus". This is usually somewhat quieter, but above all much more manageable than LHS 3447 in terms of distances. Asellus cmdrs usually start on a planetary surface.

The procedure in the station is the same at all starting points: After selecting 'launch' in the menu item of the station, you nod off that you have understood the standard assignment of the keys to be detached from the landing area a moment after activating „launch" function.

At this point there is not much to explain, the menu items are largely self-explanatory and there is not much to do.

If you think it's a good idea, you can accept a possibly existing mission on the mission board for data delivery or freight delivery (please note: Your Sidewinder has only four tons of cargo capacity) to start serving the neighboring system "Eravate" (starting from LHS 3447.

Money is money, don't skip profit!

3.2 Departure

Starting from the orbital station (LHS 3447) is easy. First use the vertical thrusters upwards (default: key "R") to "free" yourself from the surrounding structures, then thrust forwards (default: key "W") to fly away from the station.

Important here: The throttle lever on the right in the central radar display. It has a blue area, which describes approximately the area of the ship's best agility.

In the immediate vicinity of a station it is not possible to start the jump drive intended for faster travel (neither to fly between the systems in the local system (the so-called "supercruise"), nor to jump to other systems (the so-called "hyperjump").

Therefore, one must first reach a certain distance from the station. The mass lock indicator is located to the right of the fuel gauge. As soon as the blue mark disappears you can start charging your frame shift drive.

When departing orbital stations, you can simply jump into supercruise of the respective system by activating the jump drive without first specifying another system as the target. It is irrelevant how the ship is aligned, after reaching full charge after activating the supercruise (standard key: "J") the ship goes directly into supercruise after a short countdown.

To jump to another system, select either a route on the galactic map or, faster and easier, a nearby system from the short menu on the left side of the ship (default key: "1").

All targets with "ly" behind the listed name (and distance) are other systems (with very few exceptions in very large systems).

After loading the jump drive (default: key "J") (yes, the same one!) you have to align it to the target system's vector first. Simply center the filled (!) sphere in the small compass located to the left of the large radar screen.

Starting from a surface settlement is not more difficult, but a bit different: there is a big planet in your way. The vertical thrusters are also used here to detach from the landing surface until one is far enough away from the buildings of the ground station.

But then you don't fly "somewhere", but at an angle of more than 60 degrees upwards.

"More than 60 degrees", as the temperature discharge of hotter ships is no longer ideal when the upper degrees are reached. This is not a problem with your starter ship, the sidewinder, but it can become a problem later, so you should get used to it right away. The difference in distance covered from the surface in the last 30 degrees (60-90 degrees) is no longer crucial so you can be "lazy".

Once you have flown out of the mass barrier of the planet, you can easily switch to the supercruise in the same system:

Standard key: press "J" to activate jump drive without target set, then use the compass to align the ship (if you are still close to the planet) with the "escape vector" from the planet attraction.

In most cases, you cannot jump directly to the desired system in the direct vicinity of the planet. The area shaded by the planet is too large. In this case please simply use supercruise (no system to choose, just activate your jump drive, fly away from the planet for a minute) to gain some distance. The further your distance the smaller they are blocked by the planetary body.

It is helpful to point about 30 degrees in any direction after reaching supercruise so that the planet is not permanently behind you - this would keep the vector "hidden" in another system, which we want to prevent.

With some distance then simply select the system (again) and jump.

If you're moving slower in normal speed range than usual, this is often due to "few PIPs in ENG"

> **Reminder: Pips = filled circles, power distributor = right of the radar: SYS, ENG, WEP, RST - adjustable with the arrow keys.**

If it still doesn't go faster ahead or if jumping into other system doesn't work (see next chapter), then most likely
- your landing gear is still extended (standard key: L)
- weapons are still extended (standard key: U)
- cargo scoop is still activated (default key: Pos1 above the arrow keys)
- or even a combination of these.

3.3 Navigation And Jumping Into The Neighboring System

To jump into a neighboring system in Elite Dangerous, opening the galactic map is actually too much effort.

It is more efficient to open the short menu for navigation: Standard key: „1"

Tab: "Navigation"
- all listed destinations marked with "Mm" for million meters or "ls" for light seconds are in the same system
- all listed targets marked with "ly" for light years are in other systems (with a few rare exceptions).

After marking the target system you simply return to the front view in the ship and load the jump drive as described in the last subchapter. When the jump drive is fully charged, you turn to the target.

Short:
- Select target
- Load jump drive
- Align to target
- Pay attention to full speed (basic condition for a successfully activated jump)

The placement of a target in the galactic map is similarly simple but takes a little more time. For a neighboring system within the (total) range of the jump drive (using multiple jumps), point the mouse pointer to the desired system and then select the route symbol (a series of "balls" along a line).

This route icon also creates routes to distant destinations. Important is not only that the range of the ship without refueling - or when using a Fuel Scoop - may not be sufficient (dotted line = no fuel in this area of the route), but also the fact that with the initially installed jump drive the Sidewinder the single-jump-range is often not sufficient to reach some systems because of an impossible routing. This only happens with very short jump ranges below 10-12 light years per jump.

For comfortable traveling, you need a ship with at least 15 light years single jump range and a Fuel Scoop that is sufficiently large. The more jump range, the better.

As described in the previous chapter, however, our first journey only takes us into the neighboring system. In the case of LHS 3447 as your starting system, we jump to Eravate, in the case of Asellus Primus the journey goes to Eranin.

3.4 Navigation To The Station

After arriving at the target system, you will be in the immediate vicinity of the main star (or the main stars if there are several).

It is wise to make reducing your thrust to 0% initially after arriving in the target system a habit (default key: "X").

This buys you a little time to orientate yourself and significantly reduces the risk of flying too close to the main star and, as a result, "falling" into its area of attraction.

After reducing the power, unless you want to refuel with the help of a fuel scoop, you immediately start turning to fly away from the main star.
Distance to the main star not only cools the ship down again, but it also allows you to accelerate. An important optimization, especially for time-consuming, repetitive jumps on longer distances.

Should one fall into the area in the direct vicinity of the main star due to carelessness or because it could not be prevented (binary or tertiary systems, unfavorable positioning after arrival), it is above all important to keep calm.

During the next 30-40 seconds of the cooling process (small blue circle below the fuel gauge) try to generate as little heat as possible: keep the current thrust setting and fly straight ahead or throttle down, don't boost, don't use weapons or similar.

The main star can and should be selected during the time waiting for the cooling process to be completed:
Default: Key "1" - Tab: Navigation - Symbol: Star

When the cooling process is complete, load the jump drive (standard: "J" key) and turn away from the main star (compass: centered. symbol: hollow) and possibly towards the appearing alignment vector (blue crosshairs in the windscreen).

"Possibly to the escape vector" because his appearance depends on the distance to the main star. If there is an escape vector, you should give it a priority, if there is none (and no message mentioning one) you are most probably outside the main star's influence. Make sure you got the main star in your back when jumping out or you'll drop in again in an instant.

When using the escape vector, the compass ball must be filled and centered as it points directly to the escape vector.

Regardless of whether you "just crashed" or not, the destination of the flight is the journey to one of the stations. If you have not accepted a mission, simply select "Russell Ring" as your target in the "Eravate" system.
If you started from Asellus Primus, please select "Azeban City" as your first destination.

In supercruise within the target system and after turning away from the main star, you initially accelerate at full throttle.

On the one hand, this provides limited protection against attacks by pirates, on the other hand, it makes sense to save time: The proximity to the main star causes low speed and low acceleration capacity.

The target should then be activated:
Default key: "1" - Tab: Navigation (all destinations with "ls" as a distance unit are in the same system) From the displayed "ls destinations" please select "Russell Ring" (started in LHS 3447) or "Azeban City" (started in Asellus Primus) as the destination.

To return to the normal field of view please use the compass (to the left of the radar screen): A filled ball means "target ahead" - an empty ball means "target behind the ship". Please simply center the filled ball.

Tip:

Alignment, no matter on which target, is often easiest for beginners by first rolling (rotate clockwise or counterclockwise, mouse or stick/controller right or left) until the target is up or down in the compass (or for ships: in the radar screen), then simply pull (if up) or press (if down) to center.

When approaching in supercruise between the individual planets (and other objects) it is important to stay away from mass of any kind, because it slows you down.

In the hologram left of the radar screen, you can already see the representation of the station in supercruise. There are five types of orbital stations at this time:

1. Asteroid Bases
A rare type of station, mostly poorly equipped and somewhat hidden, but in any case with enormous flair and atmosphere. Worth a visit. During the approach, it is important to know that there is only one entrance. However, this is clearly visible on the left hologram when on the correct side of the asteroid.

2. Outposts
These look in some way like a collection of shoe boxes that are somehow connected to each other. Special features of outposts are quickly explained: lack of parking space and lack of security. Parking spaces are scarce, so you should try to keep your docked phases short when playing in open mode. Other players waiting for you to undock may become hostile if you go to the fridge in the back of your spaceship for some ice cold Gerasian Gueuze Beer...

Outposts are not capable of defending you against mighty pirates. They might chase away an NPC, but they won't kill a human killer out for prey. Your only way of protection near an outpost is either running away or docking. The latter is 100% safe if you're fast.

3. Coriolis
These stations are based on the geometric figure of a dodecahedron, a shape with 12 surfaces. This type originates from the initial version of Elite (1984). Actually, it corresponds in all its characteristics to the other large station types, but has two special features: The entrance is not clearly visible by observing the station's shape and Coriolis type stations can come with centrifugal pods (which are quite dangerous when rammed. Be advised that the outer arms of these travel at quite some velocity with a huge mass. They're like Thor's hammer in some way). To find the entrance, you simply fly closer than 7.5 km to the station and apply for clearance to land (Standard: Taste »1« ? Contacts ? Station name ? Landing clearance).

After receiving landing clearance, you can see „arrows" on the station's hologram left of your radar screen. Use them, they're more than helpful in finding the entrance.

4. Megaship
These are basically giant ships, not stations. Nearest megaship near Eravate is not for regular use but used for detention. You can either become a (caught) criminal to visit it or just simply fly to „Mercy's Hammer" in „ALRAI SECTOR KH-V B2-7" (5.17 ly away).

5. Orbis and Ocellus Stations
Ball on a stick style. This object is the hangar area of the station and should be approached, the only entrance is an extension of the longitudinal axis. Orbis and Ocellus are the easiest stations to fly to.
All the major stations - Coriolis, Orbis, and Ocellus - have one thing in common:

The main entrance is always located towards the planet. Valid for all stations with an adjacent planet, which is the norm.

Towards the planet, in this case, does not mean "aiming exactly at the planet", but "generally towards the planet" with an inclination of 30-60 degrees away from it.

The basic rule valid in earlier versions of Elite and before the introduction of the direction arrows at Coriolis stations was: "into the gap between planet and station, then towards station". This rule is still a good starting point for a meaningful approach, as it positions one near the main entrance after transitioning to the normal speed range by dropping near the station.

3.5 Approach And Landing

If you have successfully switched to normal speed range after approaching in supercruise, you are near the station, but not close enough for the landing clearance. The lower limit for requesting clearance is a 7.5 km distance.

First, you fly in the direction of the station in order to get a landing clearance at a distance of fewer than 7,5 km. If this is given (one sees the allocation message of the landing area above the radar screen) check for the main entrance on Coriolis stations by looking at the left hologram's arrows.

With ocellus and orbis type station just fly to the outer surface of the "node" or „ball" an extension of the main axis. At asteroid bases towards the (hopefully) indicated entrance and at outposts simply generally towards the station.

The speed should be reduced to 100 m/s or less from a distance of approx. 5 km at the latest - the danger of accidentally ramming a computer-controlled ship is too great. If that happens, you get a fine. If the other ship is destroyed, the station starts shooting at you without delay. With small ships, a single shot (!) is usually enough to destroy the ship.

It should be mentioned here that while Elite has one of the most pleasant, educated, polite and altruistic "communities" in the games/simulation world, as in real life, there are people in Elite whose purpose in life is to inflict pain and torture on others with a joyful bonus in ridiculing their victims on twitch or youtube.

One of their methods to achieve this is to make a small and easily destructible ship as invisible and fast as possible and then ram large and expensive ships approaching a station, which inadvertently fly over 100 m/s fast. First, the small ship is destroyed by the ram, then the station opens fire on the "evil, big and much too fast ship" - and destroys it, too. In the balance, the creature that finds fun in making life difficult for others has to bear the damage of a few thousand credits for his small disposable ship. The "commander" of the other ship, who is actually innocent but traveled a few m/s too fast, "may" not only "carry" the replacement value of his large ship, but also his freight, his not yet cashed in bounties or the mission freight - often amounting to several million credits.

Notice:

Near the station 100m/s or less. Without exception!

When flying into larger stations, caution is also advised: If the speed is reduced too quickly, this can quickly lead to "rear-end collisions" in the "open" game mode.

At the end of this section, two special features should be mentioned.

On the one hand the issue of assigned landing pads being occupied by NPC.

This mistake has been a "running gag" (more: a nuisance) in Elite for years, which occurs more and more rarely, but obviously cannot be completely eliminated due to Elite's current networking concept. A wise newbie I once taught me explained it was part of his role play: Even in the year 330x there are people parking in a reckless manner.

It can happen that after entering the station in the open game mode you spot a ship – quite often a Beluga - on the assigned landing pad. Please do not try to land next to or on this ship (and DO NOT open fire at it!), but turn around, fly out of the station, cancel the existing landing clearance at a safe distance and request a new clearance. If this procedure does not lead to success after the 2nd or 3rd time, please fly out of the station and switch to "solo" play mode. Once you have docked while in solo mode, you can return to open mode and continue playing normally.

The reason for this glitch is an error in coordinating players' instances to one commonly shared one. This is particularly the case when at peak times you have to resort to suboptimal pairings between internet connections.

On the other hand, there is the matter of damage to one's own ski, be it due to thermal overheating or a fight.

It may happen that the station does not appear in the standard menu for landing clearance requests. This is not an error in the program, but is due to a defective sensors module (which also works as a communication transmitter, obviously): Standard: Key "4" ? Modules: In the window, there the module package "Sensors" is almost certainly at 0% and thus completely in the bucket.

The remedy is a reboot/repair - to be called up in the right window (default: key "4" ? Functions: At the bottom.)

Please don't be afraid, during the restart of the ship there's a nose full of oxygen from your space helmet, because during the restart all systems go down and up again, even the regular ship life support.

3.6 At The Destination

If you are docked at another station for the first time, it is helpful to know a bit about the station's menu structure. So here are the most important things about "In the station".

First of all, an important thing: You don't (!) have to use the "hangar" to do essential things. Nor does the hangar help to improve the lack of parking space at small stations.

The "Hangar" function is actually just a gimmick: If you select ship equipment, the ship automatically goes "below deck" anyway, and the hangar offers neither more protection nor more functions, it's simply time-consuming.

> **Tip:**
>
> Don't use hangar mode – it's a waste of time.

The main screen of the station is roughly divided into three parts.

On the left-hand side you can see:

- Commodities Market
- Mission Board
- Passenger Lounge
- Contacts
- Universal Cartographics
- Crew Lounge

1. Commodities market

The commodities market is the main point of contact for traders or during missions involving the importation of goods. In addition to the prices for purchasing and selling goods, you can also find the quantities available for purchase or the demand for a certain commodity.

It is helpful to know that although many stations do not indicate any demand, they may nevertheless accept delivered goods, sometimes at high prices. So you can't rely on "no demand" if in doubt check it.

In the commodities area, it is interesting to display the profit of a good in relation to delivery to or delivery from a particular system in the column to the right.

2. Mission Board

The missions are assigned by individual "small factions" that are located in the current system. The availability of the missions depends on a variety of factors. For you, as a beginner lay emphasis on the wealth of the system and the possibilities of your ship, then on your ranks (which is the slowest lever in creating better missions as improving ranks takes the most time).

he system in which you accept missions should be as large as possible and as populated as possible. Populated in terms of NPC inhabitants and populated in terms of „human" traffic. It is also of advantage if a richer form of economy is present. Ultimately, the state of the system and of its small factions also influence the type and number of missions offered, and thus the potential income from them.

Your ranks are a factor for more lucrative missions. With increasing ranks in combat (attack missions and combat missions) in trade (trade missions) and exploration (primarily passenger missions that benefit), the missions offered become more lucrative, but also more difficult.

Your ship is - of course - an important factor: large ships cannot land on small outposts, ships without cargo space are not suitable for delivering goods.

Beginners are urgently advised to do simple missions, for example, to deliver data or goods to another system. This not only provides the broadest margin of error, but it also helps a lot in ranking up as this is not linked to difficulty but solely to the shown number of plus symbols at REP quality of a mission. Please always read through everything in detail and consider whether the expenditure of time is worth it. Distance to a target system and to target station and legal status are just a few things to consider each time you accept a mission.

> Tipp: For beginners, there is a small bonus in the mission board - a (simple) 10,000 credits mission.

3. Passenger lounge

Passenger missions are among the most lucrative sources of revenue. It is important that you read the descriptions well and, for example, only transport criminal subjects if you have a little experience in "smuggling" when approaching stations. Otherwise, a lucrative mission quickly turns into a costly nightmare.

(Smuggling is easy. When approaching a station, check you don't use vector thrusts and don't turn hard. Don't pitch hard. Don't boost hard. Don't even think hard. Whenever you see the huge „scan detected" message in your windscreen, drop a heatsink. Hard. Just kidding. Low temperature near 0% = Scan fails. Use 2 heatsinks to keep the temperature down over a long time without being warm enough for getting scanned in between. Once inside the station, you're safe.)

Passengers can be helpful to increase the trading rank (normal passenger missions) or the exploration rank (tourism missions) while earning a lot of money at the same time. Those who call the "Horizons" package their own will quickly discover that passenger missions with planetary surfaces as a target are particularly lucrative.

4. Contacts

The "Contacts" section is divided into up to five sections.

a) Authority Contact is the place to go whenever you wish to do anything bounty related, be it paying off a bounty (or a fine) on your own head or cashing in on earned bounties after destroying culprits' ships.

b) Combat Bond Contact is where you can cash in on military bonds. Money earned for one of the minor factions in a conflict zone after pledging to it temporarily on location (in conflict zone).

c) Power Contact is your powerplay character's local minion's office. Go there to cash in on powerplay income.

d) Search And Rescue Contact should be used to cash in on „rescued" stuff like escape pods you collected outside missions. Collecting (Scavenging) can be a lucrative hobby for lower ranked cmdrs. Just search for degraded signal sources (visit and scan the local nav beacon, then use left in ship navigation to find degraded mission sources of threat 0 or 1).

e) Black Market: Stations that allow black market trading (some government structures like „corporation does not) do have an active black market button. You can sell stolen or illegal goods there. If not stolen but just illegal, black markets are either used to weaken a controlling faction's influence or for... earning money. The latter is only making sense when selling at stations with a high demand on what you sell. War plagued stations might have a certain interest in forbidden weapons for example...

A sixth button might be present at certain stations, called „Material Trader". This is a functionality of the „horizons" package for trading in certain collected materials (or data). Useful only if you use horizons, wish to engineer and got a demand for a certain material you can't find and wish to trade in for another.

5. Universal cartographics

The cartography area is the place where you sell your collected exploration data.

Take into account that your starter ship, a "Sidewinder" is capable of many tasks you don't even think about, yet. There's a natural inner urge to „buy a bigger ship, a better ship, not that starter thing", but even a sidewinder can do quite some stuff in space.

Every sidewinder has a built-in scanner for planetary systems, a so-called D-scanner.

Each time you enter a system, this scanner automatically scans the systems close to you. This provides a small but steadily growing library of star systems (which are lost in case your ship gets destroyed, so cash in on them in short intervals).

By assigning your d-scanner to a fire button and using it in exploration mode while traveling somewhere, you not only gather information about the stars close to you but about all objects in your current system. The resulting bonus income is something you will enjoy, promised.

6. Crew Lounge
allows you to hire pilots for your ship launched fighter(s) – Horizons' content.

IN THE MIDDLE:

GALNET

Galnet is totally independent, totally uninfluenced and utterly honest... just kidding.

Galnet is a wild collection of more or less interesting news in the elite world. From the PR-suited self-congratulation of player groups to global news or the latest gossip about Thargoids - here you will find what you are looking for.

Uninteresting? No way! Above all the statistics to be found here are worth gold if you wish to influence (local) politics or do powerplay.

ON THE RIGHT:

Holo Me [HORIZONS]
Livery
Fuel / Repair / Restock
Remote workshop [HORIZONS]
OutfittingShipyard
Advanced Maintenance

1. Holo Me [HORIZONS]

A detailed menu to change the appearance of your "commander".

It is amazing how many (pictured female) avatars got a quite masculine voice in chat later on...

2. Livery

The exterior paintwork of the currently used ship with all available accessories. Often, there is truth to „Less is more", though. Some player ships only have a distant resemblance to a spaceship – but generally, everything YOU like is allowed. It's your ship, Cmdr!

3. Fuel / Repair / Restock

A very important menu item. Do yourself a favor and make it a habit to stop by here - directly after each landing. There is a huge annoyance factor in not having refueled or repaired your ship or – may the void be with you – not restocking your ammo.

4. Remote Workshop [HORIZONS]

If you have engineers available for ship tuning (Horizons package), you can order improved modules "by remote control" here, after having been with the respective engineer and bookmarking your "favorite improvement" with him.

5. Outfitting

Here you will find all possible modules for your ship. Modules are marked in sizes (numbers from 0 to 8) and in qualities (A to E)

Equipping ships is far more complex than could be dealt with in this subchapter. Please refer to the corresponding chapter of the respective module (chapter Modules 6.2. and SubItems) before using the Outfitting section.

> **Important:** Not every station has a full range of all conceivable modules. The richer and larger the system you are in and the greater its technology orientation, the more likely it is that larger and more expensive modules will be in stock.

6. Shipyard
As with the outfitting option, ships are not available everywhere. Sidewinders or other small ships are available at (almost) every station with a shipyard.
Larger ships are only offered at rich, large, technology-oriented stations. Some ships' availability depends on other factors like political orientation, too. Anyone who – for example - wants to buy an imperial ship at a Federation station has not really understood the political landscape inside Elite, yet.

7. Advanced maintenance
Besides the menu item regarding fuel, repairs and restocking advanced maintenance is another very important menu item. Do yourself a favor and make it a habit to stop by directly after each landing for maintenance as well as fuel and co.

4. Navigation

You already got to know the simplest form of navigation during the "First Flight" chapter - simply open the left cockpit window (standard key: "1") and select a nearby destination, which can be recognized by the abbreviation "ly" (light year) behind the name.

This short list is particularly useful for missions or general short-range travel in the vicinity of a faction - when dealing with nearby systems. Unfortunately, it only shows targets in the range of 15 - 19 lightyears maximum (it is limited to a certain amount of entries.
Unfortunately, this maximum display is not influenced by the ship or the "commander", but by the number of reachable systems. If one is surrounded by many nearby systems, the range is reduced by limiting the maximum jump targets.

The Galactic Map (chapter 4.2.1.) can be used for routes, especially to systems further away. In addition to route planning for routes of up to 1000 (!) light years, there are also various options for extending your range or optimizing the route.

Due to the long loading time and the countless options, these maps should not be used for short distances.

If your range is not sufficient, there are different possibilities of improvement without buying parts of the ship.

4.1 Jump Range And Equipment

Two factors are crucial for traveling, whether it's about short or long distances. The greatest possible single jump distance and the question of whether the fuel is sufficient for the whole distance or how to refuel on the way.

Your ship's jump range can be influenced by the "commander" a lot. Two things are important: the quality of the "FSD" jump drive and the weight of the ship.

With the "FSD" jump drive, the largest possible module should always be used. Simply use the largest number available as your FSD's module class.

If a class "3" slot for a jump drive is possible, this class should be used without exception, all smaller classes are much too weak.

In addition, the "FSD" Jump Drive always uses the module quality that can be afforded - even if the section on ship outfitting says otherwise with regard to modules, this does not apply to the "FSD" Jump Drive: those who want range simply buy the most expensive.

The jump drive itself compensates for the high weight of itself in case you select a heavy FSD module.

The second decisive factor for the maximum single jump distance after the FSD is the total weight of the ship.
It helps immensely not to use the heavy module qualities "E" and "B". "E"-modules because they are simply bad in performance regarding weight, "B"-modules because their weight has an enormous impact and the jump range deteriorates massively.

If you want to achieve a maximum range, select "D" modules (memory hook: D = diet), or possibly "A" modules of a class that is one or two levels below the maximum possible size. Be careful though: smaller classes can cause problems, too small shields, for example, do not cover the whole hull. There's damage to the hull, even though the shields are intact!

Often it is not the jump range for the individual jump that is the limiting factor, but the total range. Some ships provide ranges of 150-200 light-years, others have already exhausted their maximum range (their fuel capacity) after 2-3 jumps.

It is therefore also important to increase your ship's total range. This can be achieved by installing additional tanks. The increased weight due to the fuel on board again reduces the single jump range, which we have just increased... It is, therefore, better to use a Fuel Scoop as already described in chapter 2. Fuel tanks should only be used to make sure you can jump several times when inside neutron fields or other places with no scoopable main stars present, e.g. on longer exploration trips.

4.2 Longer Distances

If you want to cover longer distances, i.e. more than 1-2 jumps in a "known and populated" area, Elite has powerful functions including a very fast and reliable route planner inside the Galaxy map functionality.

The Galaxy map contains plenty of information, much more than can be described here for beginners.

4.2.1 The Galactic Map

This chart is available on the left ship menu (default key: "1"). It is THE ONE tool par excellence for any journey beyond 10-15 light years (or beyond a single jump). For shorter distances the navigation shortlist in the same menu is sufficient.

If you open the galactic map, you can see the five important tabs in the upper left corner, which are marked by symbols.

1. Lines - the description page of what is currently selected.

Here you can see all relevant data of the respective system at a glance. Important is above all the star class (only KGBFOA and M are "grateful for scooping", you remember the sentence from above), the population size, the condition, and the economy. In addition, this view shows which of your ships are parked in the system.

2. Route - (line with points) The page to create routes

Here you can easily display a route to a destination. Simply enter the exact destination system (take care about blanks in between and the difference between 0 and O (zero and „o"). Fill this system name into the search area and let it do its job of finding stuff, then point with the mouse pointer at the system in the map and create a route with the route symbol available there.

> **CAUTION!**
> **Routes displayed with (partially) dotted lines mean "NOT enough fuel"**
> **Use a fuel scoop**

Without refueling mid route or the use of a fuel scoop, a visit to the website of the "Fuel Rats" for a reserve canister could become necessary.

Using section "jump data" you normally choose "Fastest routes" because the economical routes setting creates disproportionately longer routes with a lot more jumps and time needed. Only if you do not want to use a fuel scoop or in case you want to explore an area more closely, you should choose the "economical" setting here.

FSD Boost function is described later with Horizon's synthesis function: you can produce a clearly higher jump range using specially manufactured fuel for a jump. This should be reserved for emergencies, as collecting the necessary materials is quite time-consuming.

The control slider "mass" is normally set by the existing freight itself, but it can be helpful in certain situations, which are not dealt with here. It simply simulates the presence of cargo.

4. Bookmarks - The list of already set bookmarks - to search and manage

Bookmarks are not only useful as... bookmarks. They also affect the display of the map itself. If you fly to systems more often, you should bookmark them for this reason alone: The system is then safely displayed in the map and not ignored as "unimportant".

5. Stars - The symbol for adjusting the map display

This tab is divided into three sections.

The *REALISTIC* tab has no further options, it is simply the clearest representation of the individual systems without much additional information. Possible jumps, bookmarks, ships, community goals - everything you need at a glance. It's a good choice.

The *MAP* division is exactly the opposite: Here, the card can be linked with all kinds of data, for example, to show trade routes for import or export. Simply select the desired product and link it to the import or export price. Trade routes can also be very helpful here.

A lot of other information, not only about trading is available here, please have a look at the options in case you are looking for something one day. This map view is very powerful.

The *POWER PLAY* section shows all necessary information about the power areas of the Powerplay characters. their extent, which systems are controlled or exploited, their headquarters, etc.

Server - options to display the map in the map view

This tab allows you to selectively disable the markers on certain systems. Of course, other symbols are important for Explorer than for dealers.

4.2.2 The System Map

The system map also has tabs to change appearance:

1. Overview
Everything relevant in a system in one view: Political and economic factors including influence, political affiliation, and systems, the status of all minor factions. You can switch from a schematic view to an orrery projection showing planetary objects in a 3D to 2D projection. Astronomy buffs will love it.

2. Lines
This tab shows more detailed information about a selected object. For planetary objects, for example, the physical data, which can be very helpful for planned landings or finding materials for Horizons' engineers. At stations, it shows all relevant economic data and the ownership situation.

3. Bookmarks

This tab shows all bookmarks set in the system.

4. Targets

In this tab, you get a list of all known approachable structures, stations, ground stations, and landable planets.

4.2.3 The Planet Map

The planet map corresponds mostly to the system map, just on a planetary level.

4.2.4 Neutron Stars

If you need to get from A to B quickly - or simply don't enjoy hours of jumping - you can activate the use of neutron stars in route planning.

Depending on the route and the jumping ability of the ship, you can save a lot of time by using the neutron stars to increase the jump range by 50-100% per jump.

BE CAREFUL, THOUGH!
Using the neutron star catapult is always associated with damage and often with destructive danger!

In order to use a neutron star to increase the range despite all warnings, one first positions oneself at a safe distance and looks at the monster at rest.

Neutron stars have a double tail that exits at opposite "poles". The aim is to bring one's own ship "into the flow" by aligning it POINTING AWAY FROM THE STAR somewhere halfway out from it. Don't get too close and don't go perpendicular.

For this purpose, one flies slowly and carefully into the outer districts of the tail. It is important to fly in carefully with an orientation that always points away from the star and always remains outside the inner area. You don't want to fall in and fight with all the heat and radiation, you just want to use the tail for a bit more jump range.

Once in the tail, the swell becomes significantly rougher and the message from the FSD jump drive "outside specifications" is shown to you. Now please open the galaxy map without hectic, but without delay and select a route with a neutron star.

After that, the jump drive is started and off we go with the extra mile available.

> And here again, **CAUTION**. Using neutron windows has already caused a lot of frustration. Use is never 100% safe, especially if you don't use a genuine neutron star but one of the white dwarfs which not only gives you less additional jump range than a „pristine neutron" but also more potential trouble.

4.3 Nitromethane Injection [horizons]

Of course, there is no nitromethane in Elite Dangerous. But admit it, that was a "take a look" magnet.

What there is, is the possibility to synthesize "fuel" for the jump drive. This does not replace real fuel but is more some kind of „magic additive" that provides 25%, 50% or even 100% more range for ONE jump, depending on level (1-3).

This method of increasing your range is harmless and can neither be associated with damage nor with spontaneous self-destruction - in contrast to the neutron star method.
To increase the range, open the right in-ship window (standard key: "4") and select the second lowest side tab in the form of a honeycomb structure under "Inventory".

Under "FSD INJECTION" you will find the three available levels.

Here comes the catch: The necessary materials must have been collected beforehand, in the case of the highest range level even rare materials such as yttrium and polonium. These "high-grade" materials are hardly available without Horizons, which means that this form of increasing reach is de facto reserved for the "privileged", the owners of the "Horizons" package.

5. Income And What To Do Best For Beginners

Basically Elite is not an MMO, but a huge "sandbox" simulator. Since this must get along however without "God mode", earning money is an important factor.

If you are happy about the first million at the beginning and a Sidewinder that is quite well equipped with it, be advised this is only a minuscule portion of the wealth you need to gather for the bigger ships: there is no real limit to the expenses in the ship sector: a fully equipped battle corvette quickly costs a billion (!) credits or more.

The good news is that income is rising fast. While you possibly have trouble earning 100,000 credits per hour in the beginning, more and more sources of income open up over time, which eventually leads to 20-100 million credits per hour. (Greedy? Check CORE MINING howtos on youtube or read the mining chapter!)

If you want to do yourself a big favor, please don't consider Elite a game and certainly not one with an endgame. It's a vast simulator and grind is death to all fun.

As a result, although all activities are carried out with maximum efficiency, the dreaded "grind" is omitted. So you arrive at money bag status a bit later and you will fly the huge ships a bit later, but to be honest: the „biggies" are no pleasure for most "commanders" anyway because they are not fast, not agile and certainly not to operate „with ease".

Keep in mind, that the bigger ships reach rebuy sums of 20-50 million credits (!) and sometimes more – which you have to pay every single time something goes really wrong.

One of the most important tips is to have fun "on the road": Setting goals but never struggling excessively for them.

5.1 Ranks, Ranks, Ranks

Ranks in Elite Dangerous have multiple meanings. Not only do they serve as targets for achievements for many people, but they also unlock systems and ships and are a prerequisite for lucrative missions.

Fun Fact: Whoever reaches an "elite" rank in one of the three areas exploration, trade or combat, gets access to Shinrarta Dezhra's Jameson Memorial Station.

There are all ships, all modules, and all weapons without much travel in one place with a 5% discount. If that's not an incentive...

5.1.1 The "Elite" Ranks

Elite Dangerous offers three "main" ranks to track your progress: Exploration, trade, and combat.

These three rank systems have one thing in common: The step in between is 100% more work for each level, i.e. Reaching rank 2 from rank 1 takes you „100" in efforts. Reaching rank 3 from rank 2 would then be „200" in efforts.

It makes sense to ensure balanced progress in the three main ranks, as all three have an influence on your offered missions. The higher the ranks the better your job offers.

5.1.1.1 Exploration

First, the exploration ranks in order:

- Aimless
- Mostly Aimless

- Scout
- Surveyor
- Trailblazer
- Pathfinder
- Ranger
- Pioneer
- Elite

In the past, one could roughly estimate an income needed of about 160 million credits from sold cartographic data for reaching elite rank. This is no longer possible today, because not only the sale of the exploration data increases the exploration rank. Also, the transportation of passengers on exploration tours or on tourism missions offers a way forward here.

If you want to climb up the ranks quickly in the exploration sector, you should either travel specifically to "high-priced" systems or, even more effectively, complete passenger missions. Which of the passenger missions is more effective depends very much on what is chosen and which ship is used.

> **Important:** A healthy level of exploration rank, at least in the mid-range, is a prerequisite for getting offered the more lucrative (passenger) missions.

5.1.1.2 Trade

The ranks in order:

- Penniless
- Mostly Penniless
- Peddler

- Dealer
- Merchant
- Broker
- Entrepreneur
- Tycoon
- Elite

In the past, only trading was the measure for the achievement of elite rank with approx. 1.2 billion credits one had to earn. These days, delivery missions and passenger missions ("transport!") are now included in this total sum, so that owners of smaller ships, in particular, can expect more progress from high income in the mission area than from "simple" trade routes.

An at least middle trade rank is a prerequisite for better-paid trade missions.

5.1.1.3. Combat

The combat rank is of great importance. Not only does it have the most prestige in encounters with other "commanders", but it is also immediately displayed in the info window. It also has the greatest influence on the allocation of combat missions.

But the most important thing about your combat rank is that it determines the strength of your regular computer opponents!

Outside of missions where the opponent strength largely depends on the mission, combat rank controls the "random" encounters with bad boys (and to some degree the spawn in resource zones, too). If you want to be civic and want to avoid fighting in general, you should try to keep your fighting rank as low as possible, so please act completely against the recommendations below!

The ranks in order:

- Harmless
- Mostly Harmless
- Novice
- Competent
- Expert
- Master
- Dangerous
- Deadly
- Elite

Combat rank is increased by destroying ships in combat - exclusively ships steered by computer opponents. Destroying ships of other "commanders" does not contribute to combat rank.

The better the opponent's combat rank is - in relation to your own combat rank, the higher the bonus achieved.

Examples:
As "Commander" of the Combat Rank "Competent" you are attacked by a computer opponent who is also classified as "Competent". Destroying it creates a combat rank bonus of "1". If you destroy a computer opponent of rank "Deadly" with your own combat rank being "Competent", you get a bonus of "2" as your opponent is „way above your league".

If you are attacked having a rank of "Competent" by an opponent rated as "Harmless" and you win the battle, you only get a bonus of "0.25" as a harmless NPC is considered „a piece of cake" for you being „Competent" in rank.

Anyone wishing to increase their fighting ranks should, therefore, go to places where high-ranking targets are to be found, such as "hazardous" mining areas (resource zones).
But beware: there is no support by security forces and the opponents are hardly controllable for beginners. For now, keep it slow and easy...

Fun Fact: There are so-called "compromised" navigation beacons, where the same criminals romp about, who otherwise can only be found in the "hazardous" mining areas (resource zones), but here without the disturbing obstacles, safer and more effective to „harvest" rank.

Unfortunately, there is no clear rule for finding these "compromised" beacons. But if you encounter one while traveling, you should perhaps remember its location for later visits.

5.1.1.1.4. CQC / Arena

This rank has no significance for the mission assignment and is not a "real" elite rank. It arises from the achieved rank within the game-in-game addition "CQC" or "Arena", an arcade fun in which you compete against each other with small ships. Those who like arcade style gaming can spend a really good and eventful time in CQC/Arena, it is basically complex „ELITE: Dangerous" reduced to small ship pewpew.

5.1.2 The Military Ranks

Two of the three major political factions have a military force to "protect" their own interests: The Federation and the Empire.

Their military ranks partially enable access to certain systems. As an example, access to the Federation's rank "Petty Officer" provides access to SOL – the origin of mankind.

In addition, reaching certain ranks is necessary for unlocking certain ships. The Imperial Clipper as an example needs you to be ranked "Baron" in the Empire's Navy.

The significance of the individual ranks cannot be judged objectively since they are of different importance for each individual "commander": For some, the visit of "SOL" is of highest personal importance, for others the acquisition of the Imperial Cutter as an armed XXL freighter is a personal goal.

Ranks of the Federation and what you get for it

- Recruit
- Cadet
- Midshipman... Federal Dropship
- Petty Officer ... Access to SOL
- Chief Petty Officer ... Access to "VEGA" & "BETA HYDRI" & Federal Assault Ship
- Warrant Officer ... "PLX 695"
- Ensign ... "ROSS 128" & Federal Gunship
- Lieutenant ... "EXBEUR"
- Lieutenant Commander
- Post Commander ... "HORS"
- Post Captain
- Rear Admiral ... Federal Corvette
- Vice Admiral

- Admiral

Ranks of the Empire and what you get for it

- Outsider
- Serf
- Master ... Imperial Courier
- Squire ... "ACHENAR"
- Knight
- Lord
- Baron ... "SUMMERLAND" & Imperial Clipper
- Viscount
- Count
- Earl ... "FACECE"
- Marquis
- Duke ... Imperial Cutter
- Prince
- King

5.2 Missions

As we already mentioned earlier, Elite Dangerous is NOT a classic MMO or even a "quest" based game with refined gameplay.

Nevertheless, it is important to be familiar with the missions offered. It also makes sense to pay attention to efficiency in completing missions when it comes to income.

The most suitable missions for beginners are delivery missions for data or small quantities of goods to neighboring systems. Both variants are only slightly dangerous. They deliver only small rewards, but they are also quickly done.

You should definitely keep your fingers off the delivery missions with larger quantities before you reach the 100-ton freight class. Although a lot is paid, the mission duration is can accumulate into hours.

Attack missions, military missions, and other "active" missions are also not worth mentioning when it comes to effectiveness in small ships. Apart from that, the enemies in these missions are only conditionally adapted to their own combat rank and experience. The probability of losing your ship is much higher.

5.2.1 Introduction to the World of Missions

Effectiveness in missions means two things: maximum income and/or maximum progress in reputation or influence.

aIn general, it is very important to maximize the loyalty of the small factions of a station you are using. "Wandering Commanders" experience the constant problem of their reputation never exceeding average values wherever they go as all of their actions do dissipate on lots of different stations. This significantly reduces the range of lucrative missions on offer in comparison to a station where persistent working on one's reputation has maximized loyalty of the mission giving factions.

It is therefore advisable to choose a "home base". Those who regard their own income as the main motivation for working with missions are most likely to be at home in systems with a large population (and player traffic) and a rich economy (service, high technology) as these systems usually got the best paying missions and a broad variety of them on the stock.

Under no circumstances should you choose a starter system as your home. Although the number of "colleagues" is the highest there, unfortunately, newcomers are usually so overwhelmed with the basics of flying, navigating and staying alive that communication hardly takes place. On the other hand, the number of people of the "My goal in life is to see other players suffer"-kind is the highest there. Starter systems are hazardous places. Beware.

Systems that are 2-3 Sidewinder jumps away from the starter systems are ideal. There are occasional encounters with other players, but the number of psychopathic serial killers is significantly lower there.
Popular systems around Eravate are YAKABUGAI with its main station SEREBROV for the "more civilian" among the "commanders" and KREMAINN with its main station WOHLER for the more battle-oriented "commanders".

Those who are undecided as to what they will work towards in the long term may be satisfied with LTT 15574 and the main station HAXEL PORT. All three systems have proper station equipment and enough "old hands" who can be asked for help if something gets stuck.

If you are more anxious, you should either stay in Elite's SOLO mode or use the MOBIUS group. More about all this in chapter 8 "Finding a connection".

In your chosen "home system" you at first select missions whose "REP" value is given with as many "+" symbols as possible, ideally with the maximum number: Five.

REP – respectively your reputation with the mission giving small faction – quickly increases. After reaching the highest popularity, this leads not only to a better parking lot (no kidding! No sharp turns after entering a station anymore!) but above all to a larger amount of missions offered – all of them with increased income.

When your reputation is at a maximum, take care not to "screw up" any more missions or not to exceed the time limit of missions, because otherwise, you might lose quite some of your reputation. Every failed or expired mission lowers your reputation (and damages the mission giver's influence in the system to some degree).

If you want to support a small faction, you can either choose missions whose INF has a maximum count of „+" characters as possible (maximum: 5), or at least the variant with the highest number. This will raise the giving minor faction's influence in the system (and it will influence the targetted minor faction whenever you go somewhere to accomplish the mission. If that's of importance for you, just consider what a real-life mission of this kind would do to the place you do whatever you were told.)

As the Sidewinder is a small ship with low cargo capacity and – in comparison to larger ships – weak combat capabilities, it is highly recommended to choose simple missions: Freight deliveries of smaller quantities to nearby systems or data deliveries that require no freight capacity at all. These missions are surprise-joined - if at all - only by weaker NPC pirates and usually don't use much time. Even if the income per mission is not very high, the income per hour is sufficient, because the mission duration is very short and the perils of space are less than on well-paid missions.

Combat missions are generally not a good idea in Sidewinders. In the beginning, Elite more or less takes care about you in the form of some kind of puppy protection: your combat rank directly influences the kind of NPC opponents you will encounter. Unfortunately, this is not a set rule when doing missions so there is a considerable chance you encounter some meal you can't swallow. Feeling lucky? Try it. Just don't complain after being shot to pieces :-)

In "big small ships" (sic!) like the Cobra Mk III, the Viper Mk III or even the Vulture, combat missions are an interesting way to earn money with more "action" involved.
A Cobra Mk III is capable of destroying the largest computer-controlled ships. Not guaranteed each time you try it, not without an interesting repair bill and it will definitely take some time, but with some skillful flying involved it is a feasible thing.

> **Notice:**
>
> **Fighting in Elite is above all a question of know-how, not only in flying itself but also in the choice of ship modules and armament.**

If you do can't locate your mission objective or the place you have to go in order to find out where to go, it generally makes sense to fly to the local nav beacon near the main star. Once there, just look for a grey-white radar contact near the navigation point/radio beacon tag, this is the actual device/satellite. If you lock on it as a target using the „Target ahead" function (default: key "T"), you will receive any necessary data after a few seconds. (Grey dots can't be targetted by simply cycling through targets (default: key „G") - you need to aim visually and use „target ahead".

If you want to find a destination near a planet or another landmark, it makes sense to look at the short list of navigation destinations within a radius of 1000ls. The mission goal is usually listed here as a signal source in blue color, designated as a mission objective.

5.3 Combat And Survival

Elite Dangerous' marketing was quite clear about a „life in a cutthroat galaxy". While this is clearly an exaggeration of the real situation in the game, it is nevertheless important to deal with "eating and being eaten" in the 34th century.
The top two rules for combat and survival in Elite Dangerous are:

1. A good neighborhood

The place you are and the conditions around you are not only important when encountering computer opponents. You can keep the more dangerous computer opponents off your back simply by not flying into the „hazardous" resource zones and military conflict zones.

Danger avoidance against human players is less about locations inside systems in general, but avoiding certain system types: Aggressive human players are usually found found in the starter systems (which unfortunately speaks volumes about these people's character), at active community goals (not much better but they can claim to „play the game" there) and at engineer bases (more proficient „victims" for them there, but still questionable as people flying to an engineer most often arrive in travel configuration and being less equipped for combat).

Going to these places you should consider using SOLO game mode for your own safety. Use open only if you can afford the rebuy sum and the frustration that comes with losing a ship in a fight you can't wing.

2. Not fighting can make you a winner

At first, this seems contradictory as a fight is per definition is done to see who's got the bigger... carrot in the fridge.

At a second glance and taking into account that some fights are started in situations one of the participants has next to no chance of winning the duel, things become more complex:

When attacked by a vastly superior ship or even a group of combat ships capable to end you in no time at all, surviving can be defined as winning.

When you can't win, it's wiser and more sensible to avoid a fight and by simply surviving, determine that you've chosen the best possible outcome: not being prey to bullies.

To learn about winning-by-survival, please consult chapter 2.6. on the survival of enemy attacks.

5.3.1 Survival

Boring, but quite important: As a few lines above, please read about surviving interdictions in chapter 2.6. Being proficient in this procedure is a solid base for surviving dangerous situations.

Secondly (repetitive, but important), there are places you should avoid in the OPEN game mode as they are magnets for a rare but present kind of „commander" who enjoy trampling on your beach castle.

The starter systems - LHS 3447 - Eravate - LHS 3006 - Asellus Primus and their immediate vicinity.
The Engineers' bases - marked in the galactic map with the somehow purple 6-cornered symbol.

Active Community objectives - indicated on the galactic map by the somehow yellow 5-cornered symbol.

The SOLO game mode is identical to OPEN game mode, except for the absence of human players. Because these are many times more dangerous and unpredictable (and often more sinister in their intentions) than computer-generated characters, SOLO game mode is a good way to play when wishing for a chilled experience or when flying a vessel with a huge rebuy or some valuable goods you can't afford losing.

A PRIVATE GROUP can be created by any "commander" to give friends the right to travel in this little "private world". Private groups are once more identical to OPEN or SOLO game mode, the only difference is that you decide which human players are allowed to play with you.

The largest PvE-only (Player vs Environment) (private) group is one called MOBIUS. Participants of this group commit themselves to a set of rules. One of the most important rules? Do not initiate any fights between players. A violation of this (and other) rules results in immediate exclusion.

MOBIUS participants are a mostly laid back, friendly and polite bunch of people. More so than the average „Cmdr" in-game, that's for sure. Their friendliness and no-attack-attitude makes most combat oriented players call them carebears, which is not only derogatory, it is simply not fitting at all.

Mobius just has another approach to Elite: Enjoy the game without „bad vibes" by human attacks. It's a gentlemen club.

If you consider Elite Dangerous more a relaxing "build and construct" game than a combat simulator, you might find „your place" in Mobius.

www.elitepve.com

Another factor in terms of survivability is your choice of ship and your ability to adapt to its strengths and weaknesses.

Slow, large ships with weak shields are much more vulnerable than smaller ships with a narrow silhouette and ships capable of high (escape) speeds.
The Cobra Mk3, for example, is a true survivor, even without engineering.

By using the „turn to the enemy, escape" procedure described at length in chapter 2.6. - turning toward the enemy, boosting behind him, forcing him into a 180 turn and therefore „buying time and distance" you can escape lost interdictions even with fast and agile attackers – with minor or no damage on your ship at all. The larger your ship, the slower your ship, the weaker its shields, the more dangerous interdictions become:

Ships like the T-7 Transporter, which is mostly used without shields for increased cargo capacity, are a real pain: It's very difficult to build up distance to the enemy (they're slow), your enemy will hardly miss it (it's huge) and the little existing (hull) protection is history in seconds.

Now, of course, you're tempted to avoid destruction by turning off the game or cutting off the Internet connection (combat logging).

Here is some **IMPORTANT** information:

The so-called "combat logging", i.e. taking oneself out of the game context, no matter in which way (exception see below) is, of course, an unauthorized intervention and can be punished by Frontier Development. This can go as far as the withdrawal of the account.

Even if you are not punished by Frontier Development, there's another caveat: Combat logging, when attacked by players, will lead to you being showcased and smeared on reddit, youtube and other places as a coward and a combat logger.

So here's important advice: In no case simply kill the task of the program or interrupt the internet connection. This feeds the ones who love to wreck your in-game reputation on the internet and boost their egos.

If it is absolutely necessary to escape in a hurry, then please use the built-in function: ESC key for opening the main menu and leave the game regularly. This function has a delay timer of max. 15 seconds and is allowed.
The built-in 15-sec exit function is part of the game mechanics and can be used at any time. When used early, it often saves you from destruction even during player attacks.

It is important to know that especially the (small) serial killer fraction among the players is disturbed by this function and will quite often try to damage your reputation. The funny thing about this is, that the self-proclaimed heroes just whine about a regular game function for it to help people evade their bullying. Laugh when you see it.

5.3.2 Combat

Combat is math.

Although this is a cruel over-simplification, whenever you are willing to put skill and situation aside, there is a really strong connection between „damage is done" and „damage capacity" of your ship.

When using similar equipment in terms of offensive and defensive powers, your personal flying skill and your capability of using your weapons and ship systems without damaging your own ship by overheating are the two most important factors.

While trying to maximize „time on target" for as much damage on your opponent as possible, you need to dodge incoming fire if possible or at least keep your defense as strong as possible.

The most important thing above all, though... is the power distributor.

The power distributor is a „core" module that controls the energy flow from your power plant to your individual modules. (Actually, the function is more complex, because it is also and above all about heat, but this is of secondary importance for you at this stage.)

In addition to the RESET (RST) function (standard key: "down arrow") for resetting the distribution to 2 of 4 maximum "PIP"s in each of the three distributed „branches" or „buckets", the power distributor also has these three further allocations:

SYS – SYSTEM:

Besides providing basic energy supply to utility modules, putting "4 PIPS into SYS" not only strengthens the shield so much that it generates 250% shield strength (starting from a base value of 100% at 0 PIPS in SYS), in addition, shields also heal faster and rebuild faster when down.

ENG – ENGINES:

"4 in ENG" not only makes your ship faster in regular cruise (without boost), it also shortens the intervals between boosts and makes your ship much more agile. Whenever you need maximum agility and speed, use 4 in ENG but do not sacrifice safety by leaving SYS unattended.

WEP – WEAPONS:

Unfortunately, unfortunately, unfortunately (did I mention what a pity that is?), "4 in WEP" does not result in stronger weapons. It does enhance fire duration by recharging the „weapon bucket" more than when using fewer PIPs in WEP, though. It is also important to know that the use of weapons results in more additional heat in your ship when the "WEP bucket" is less filled than when it is near full state. That's not of much importance on smaller ships using cooler weapons as you do at your stage, but later on, you will have to manage heat in bigger ships with lots of heat sources. You need to learn to pay attention to a filled „WEP bucket" or you'll, later on, do more damage to your ship than your enemy will do.

Fights in Elite Dangerous are usually not classic "dogfights", i.e. pursuit or cornering fights, because you are - especially as a beginner - hardly able to stay behind your opponent, keeping aim, chasing his tail. Instead of continuously bringing oneself into a suboptimal fire-position and robbing oneself of all advantages by attempting a dog fight, you better consider a kind of "attack-wave-tactic" from the outset.

These attack waves, as the name suggests, are repetitive and consist of several phases:

Phase 1: Attack
One flies towards the opponent and attacks him with a previously filled „WEP" bucket. For maximum defense, while attacking, "4 PIPS in SYS" is set in order to have maximum protection against the opponent's "answer" to our attack.

The easiest thing to remember is here:
1 x arrow down + 2 x arrow left - this results in 4 PIPS in SYS and one PIP each in ENG and WEP - so nothing runs empty and you got maximum protection

During the attack phase, you should remember, especially with smaller ships, that you don't have too large shields and you should avoid enemy fire if possible – especially when fighting opponents „with bigger guns" than you got.

Dodging enemy fire is easier when you're using gimballed weapons. Using fixed weapons you need to emphasize aiming at your enemy which limits your evasive actions.

When fighting larger ships with „assault type" weapons like the dreaded large plasma accelerators (mostly found on high ranked Anaconda and Fer-de-Lance NPC), a simple trick works: During the attack phase, you simply maintain a vector thrust downwards - like when touching down on the landing pad - and rotate about 10-20 degrees to one side every 5-10 seconds.

This little "vector thrust trick" doesn't irritate your own (gimballed) weapons while firing (or only slightly), but makes it difficult for computer opponents to use plasma accelerators, cannons or rail guns on you. Please only rotate a bit every 5-10 seconds and not continuously, as the corresponding "vertical" speed must first be built up and this does not happen if you rotate continuously, too often or too harshly. Also, you should really only use shallow rolls of 10-20 degrees, because at larger angles the built up speed vector is slowed down too much.

At this point, the different range of weapons should be mentioned. With pulse lasers installed (standard equipment), keep in mind they're mostly a neat light show above 1500 meters.

Lasers generally lose punch after 500-600 meters depending on the type. They should always be used in close proximity: „Hug your enemy".

Weapons with a longer range are, for example, multi cannons, which can be used without problems up to ranges of 2500m - depending on the size of the target and its agility - without losing much of their damage abilities.

The attack phase comes to an end when either WEP is empty and no real firepower is generated anymore, you are too close to the enemy (below 500m... take care not to be rammed then) or the enemy fire is much stronger than your own.

Phase 2: Recharge and recover
Whenever you are too close to your enemy (danger of being rammed, not on target anymore) or whenever one of the other two abort criteria applies (WEP bucket empty or your opponent gives you hell in terms of damage on your side without receiving at least the same amount of beating from you), it is time to go to a safe place to recharge your power distributor, lick your wounds and possibly heal your shields with a shield cell or two.

The „I don't want to be here any longer" button is your BOOST button (default: "TAB") – please consider it your „emergency out". Make sure you do not aim directly at your opponent when pressing TAB as the boost will propel you forward and will result in a (probably) devastating ram into your enemy if you start your boost while having your enemy centered. Instead, aim somewhere besides your enemy to make sure your attempt of getting to a safe place doesn't end in a ram that damages your ship or ends the fight prematurely.

(Rams can be very useful and devastating weapons. It's just that you need to have at least the same mass of your opponent's ship and shields as strong as his for a good start. Both won't be the case in the beginning.) Your goal in using the boost is to get out of the opponent's field of fire (behind him) while not ramming him.

This procedure of „boosting behind the enemy" forces him into a 180-degree turn in order to realign himself to your new position. In the time until he has done so, you are largely protected from enemy fire (except for the few ships that use turrets, which are usually quite weak and mostly lasers. Remember 1500m on lasers for a light show without much damage due to the harsh falloff in damage done from 500-600m of distance). Depending on how much time you need, you can even boost further on a second time for a bit more distance.

As soon as you have passed your opponent on the initial boos, you immediately start to recharge your energy. First the ENG „bucket" by selecting "4 PIPS IN ENG" (1 x down arrow, 2 x up arrow) because ENG is your emergency out as described above, it provides the power for boosting and should ALWAYS be full - just in case.

As soon as ENG is full, you reload WEP in order to be able to show your opponent some affection again in the next wave.

Somewhere within this - more or less protected - time period, you might use a shield cell to heal your own shields. The larger the size number of the shield cell, the more heat is generated. So either use small shield cells or ensure that heat is dissipated by using a heat sink or an overall cool ship configuration.

The most important thing in this phase is keeping an eye on the ship's hologram on the right side of your radar screen: If you see the enemy shooting at you, select „4 PIPS in SYS" for maximum protection, even if not fully charged in ENG and WEP. Keep at least one PIP in each so they can refill until you have repositioned yourself for the next attack wave, but use maximum protection (4 in SYS) whenever under fire!)

Phase 3: Rinse and repeat

Returning to „combat", as in returning to your enemy and starting the next attack wave has no clearly defined beginning.

It starts somewhere while recharging ENG and WEP using the trigger of returning back to maneuverable speed – the blue area in your throttle/speed display.

The key point here is trying to present yourself as "flat" as possible: Most ships are relatively shallow in height and not easy to hit, especially at great distances, as long as the enemy sees them directly from the front or directly from behind. If you are outside the "blue zone" of the speed, a 180-degree turn takes much longer than inside that blue zone. During this time, even at a great distance, you are a huge, easy target to hit. Avoid that.
Therefore: At some point within Phase 2 - at your own discretion - make sure that the speed is in the blue range, then turn around to the opponent. Too early and you won't be fully recharged when under fire again – with the need of 4 in sys. Too late and you're providing healing time to your enemy in which you could long be beating him to a pulp again.

The end of Phase 3 is the start of Phase 1: Repeat your attack.

Please do not forget that survival in combat in Elite Dangerous sometimes depends on the decision whether you fight at all or whether you realize during the fight: "This has no good end, I am off!".

As a beginner you can easily set a clear limit here: If your own shields have fallen and those of your opponent have not, then it is time to leave. Now: Immediately select another system in the navigation list, load the FSD/jump drive and boost straight ahead until the jump drive is fully loaded - then turn towards the target system and boost one last time to align the ship with the direction of your target system.

This simple rule of "Shields down = get out" is only good against weak computer opponents like the one you encounter outside resource zones, conflict zones or as mission enemies.

With high ranked NPC or human – mind you: all human opponents work with lots of tricks and special tactics: They reboot your frame shift drive, raise your heat, damage your modules in no time at all and more.

The stronger the opponent, the more safety margin you should plan for.

> **Tip:** Although you'll constantly receive the BAD advice of „when attacked, do curves, lots of curves", please DON'T.

Curves make you a giant target by presenting the huge up- or downside of your ship to your attacker while giving him the opportunity to close in on you. This not only makes it easier for him to hit you in general, but it is also ideal for assassination weapons like overcharged plasmas accelerators and the like.

If you think going straight ahead is not enough and you're feeling lucky, try to tumble while boosting away. Basically, you boost with flight assist off, widen the spiral by using vector thrust downwards, sliding to one side and rotating to the other. Yes, I did not pretend it's easy. Read about this and other pro tips in the upcoming advanced part. This book's already too large for most.

In preparation for combat, there are also a few things you can do to improve your chances. Apart from pre-selecting a nearby system in your left in-ship window's navigational menu for a faster „out" if you need it, you can configure your ship in a way that a damaged power plant won't make you a sitting duck without the chance of survival. Nothing more frustrating than receiving a hit into the power plant – reducing generated power – than sitting in a dark ship, waiting for the next few shots ending you.

The right in-ship window has a tab called „modules" (standard key: "4") then "E" to select the modules page.

At first, you set all modules to value "3" - which serves as an average/base value. Then you set all modules you don't need in combat to "4" or "5" - for example, the FSD interdictor (if installed) or the cargo hatch (don't worry, you won't lose anything if you set it to "5" - it always stays closed, function is just for collecting stuff or jettisoning cargo).

Now all systems are set to an average of "3" and those not needed in combat are set to "4" or "5" - which means: "Should there not be enough power available when weapons are deployed, automagically switch these systems off and try to keep weapons in operation".

In this way, you can "overcharge" - i.e. 102% or 103% - depending on the amount of "switched off" systems. In case of overload, the unneeded (priority „4" or „5" systems simply go off once weapons are deployed).

The last step is the most important, though:
The thrusters and the jump drive are set to priority "1". If you get a hit to the power plant with shields down, these "1" set systems remain functional as power plants which have more than 0% (sic!) integrity left, still provide roundabout 40% of maximum power output. Instead of waiting in the dark ship for the finishing shot, you can get out of the mud using your „emergency power on" set thrusters and frame shift drive.

5.3.3. Earning Money: Bounty Hunting

Once you have successfully completed the first hours in your starter ship, the (in)famous Sidewinder, and you have reached some level of accommodation and general „overview" of systems and Elite's „world", you can consider doing some basic combat.

Even "commanders" who are aiming for a peaceful career are well advised to learn at least the basics of combat, even if only to better avoid it.

A good opportunity for this is to earn money by doing bounty hunting. Ships (not: commanders) that act against the law receive a bounty. These bounties are visible without additional equipment – left in ship window, contacts when having a „bad boy" targetted - if related to activity in the current system. Additional bounties „earned" in another system are not shown in the contact list.

To see (and later earn) ALL of a villain's bounties, he must be scanned with a kill warrant scanner before destruction. This increases the payout of computer opponents' rewards by 200-400% - USE IT.

Cruising in game, more than occasionally, one can see „commanders" hunting for bounty without using a kill warrant scanner. Rank progress in terms of combat rank is the same, as it is coupled to the rank of one's victim, but not so income. You are losing money when not using a kill warrant scanner!

If you wish to do bounty hunting for a living and with efficiency, do not loiter in supercruise while waiting for the occasion. Do not go to regular Nav Beacons, but follow these instructions:

Ideally - and for an income of at least 2 million credits per hour in a Sidewinder (!) do this:

1. If you are not familiar with the area you're in, use eddb.io to find out about the availability of the following module.

2. Buy a Class 0E or 0D kill warrant scanner and install it in the utility area of your ship. All utility modules are marked with size 0, the letter D or E indicates their range (E is worse/shorter), the price (D is more expensive) and the power requirement (D needs more power). After installation, please check briefly whether you have enough power to support it - either in station's outfitting or by using the right in ship window respectively its „modules" tab (standard key: "4"). In its bottom line, the electricity requirement is indicated in percent. If it is over 100% you should upgrade your power plant. After that, you have to assign it to a key that is not yet assigned to a weapon. Open the right window again and use the „fire groups" tab. Place fire button 2 on the kill warrant scanner, for example, if the weapons are already on button 1. Once you have assigned both fire buttons, you should open a new fire group: "B" - a vertical row - and place one of the buttons on the bounty scanner. Fire groups can be changed with the standard key "N", for example.

3. Go to a HIGH-intensity resource zone near you. This kind of mining area can be found in (almost) all systems in which mining and/or processing of mining products take place (mining/refinery). Just look out for planets with rings within these systems. Getting closer than 500-1000ls of distance, you will see the designated resource zones in the left in-ship window's navigational short list.
Resource zones come in different intensities. Low intensity has a weaker spawn of bad boy NPC, high intensity a more powerful one. No worries, you are not there for real fights, you are there to cash in on the police's work.

Resource zones of no detailed intensity (just „resource zone") are somewhere in between low and high-intensity zones. Use that if you got one close to you, if not please check for a high-intensity one.

„Hazardous" resource zones are not the place to go, because there's no police force present and you don't want to engage elite ranked combat ships in your sidewinder without any help, do you?

If you're not in the mood for checking neighboring systems for the availability of resource zones, simply fly to system LTT 15574 when near Eravate. It's 2-3 jumps away and is home to a station called HAXEL PORT. Haxel not only has decent traffic of real players for teaming up and well-equipped outfitting and shipyard, but there are also two high-intensity resource zones less than 100 ls away, too.

4. Make sure that you (Yes! You!) aren't wanted yourself and check your cargo hold is empty. You don't want to attract bounty hunters or pirates. Checking for „wanted" status is easy – it is shown in red letters near your fuel gauge if you are. Checking for cargo is not difficult either: just open the right i- ship window (default key: "4") and check the "inventory" tab if you have anything with you. The cargo hold should be empty, otherwise, the desire awakens in pirates, who will attack (and kill) you in no time at all.

5. Now fly to the resource zone and enter it – just approach it as if it was a station. When approaching you should make sure that you stay away from the planet and its rings for as long as possible, i.e. fly at a right angle to the rings. Both planet and rings have a large mass, which slows you down massively and ... time is money.

6. Once in the resource zone, you'll quickly feel like being part of the Elite Dangerous Teaser Trailer: Pretty asteroids everywhere.

Action? Not yet. For now, just give the system a few seconds (15-30) for spawning NPC, then check the vicinity around the resource zone's center (nav marker): Search for laser fire that looks like ongoing combat. If you see that, go there. Don't worry, without freight and not wanted there is ZERO danger for you as long as you don't shoot at someone. You'll be scanned, but largely ignored.

7. When you arrive at the fighting ships' location, switch through the targets one by one until you have found the ship with the "Wanted" tag. This is your "victim" and must first of all be scanned with the kill warrant scanner. Simply deploy your weapons and press the assigned button after targetting the wanted ship (DO NOT FIRE!) until the display shows "complete" in HUD. There's no more information in the HUD, you can only see the current bounty in the left cockpit window under "Contacts", but this is also shown after the "Kill", so save the effort for now.

8. Waiting is the most important thing in a "commander's" life: After scanning, just enjoy the show while the police give the wanted ship hell: First, its shield is destroyed, then it's all about the ship's hull. The former is shown as the blue-then-red rings at the left ship hologram, the hull's health is displayed in percent. With large ships you should wait until only 5-10% of their hull is left, with smaller ships being less sturdy, 10-20% of the hull is your „mark" from which you start to help the policemen: Shoot the ship you're looking for and don't stop until it bursts.

> Tip: Shooting at police - even if only by mistake - will make your day miserable in no time at all. With all the joy and satisfaction (sic!) to finally destroy a crippled wanted ship and earn money at the same time: Make sure no cop gets hit. Police have a hard job and tend to forget that you're firing, flying through your line of fire now and then when you don't expect it at all. So watch out!

9. <u>After destroying the wanted ship</u>, the amount you have just earned appears in blue on the top right. „Earned" is a bit much to say as the only thing you got so far is a voucher in your ship's computer which will be lost in case you get killed before cashing it in.

So please fly to the nearest station every now and then and convert the vouchers into real money under Station Services > Contacts > Authorities. The frustration of losing „earned" bounties in a mishap (firing at cops?) is huge and can spoil the fun big time.

10. <u>In order to find the next "victim"</u>, you don't just look for another combat location by searching for laser fire. After your first „kill" you instead simply follow one of the medium-speed police ships - a Python or a Viper – these scan all ships and fly toward the place of action. If you see laser fire, you can of course still fly there, maybe there are already policemen there.

> **Notice:**
>
> Under no circumstances should you use a "hazardous" resource zone (see above) – there is no police presence there and you are completely on your own. A real challenge in all small and even medium-sized ships!

After reaching a level of proficiency at which you can reliably destroy larger ships on your own, these "hazardous" resource zones begin to develop their own charm. Alternatively, you can also fly to a "compromised navigation beacon". These are about the same level of danger in terms of opponents yet without asteroids as obstacles.

5.3.4 Law And Order In Elite Dangerous

Law and order in a cutthroat galaxy. Contradictory and complex. You better know how being a bad boy is handled in Elite.

The most important thing to understand crime and punishment in Elite is the fact that legal status is not bound to a person or commander. It is bound to the ship that was used to break the law. This unusual way of handling wrongdoings might have emerged from ships being more identified more easily than a person being on board, who knows.

Let's start with the smallest violations: The newly hatched "commander" flies to a station and exceeds the 100 m/s speed limit out of pure exuberance. Strolling around and smiling from ear to ear he collides with another ship.

This results in a small fine of 50-400 credits in case of some bent metal only. This fine can immediately be paid after docking. Starport Services ? Contacts ? Authorities. No hassle.

> **Caution!**
> Collisions happen. No big deal. If you're over 100 m/s and someone's ship gets destroyed by the collision, things take a turn: The station immediately opens fire and you need knowledge, luck and a big ship to escape this inferno. Usually, you're just dead in a second.

There are larger fines for (accidental) shooting at "clean" ships without a bounty or - even worse - at law enforcement officers. Also, these fines can be paid at the station that spent the fine as long as no ship was destroyed.

> Caution though, depending on the system's security situation, the (accidental) shooting at police officers results - even with simple "fines" for just an accidental shot without "murder" - in "surrendering oneself to the police forces" instead of paying only the fine. You will soon find yourself in the nearest detention center. Not permanently, not with a time penalty but free to go. Nonetheless, this is not only humbling, but it can also be an outright nuisance if the detention center is located far out. You might have to travel back 50-80 light years because of a small issue. Fortunately, the prisons around the starter systems are numerous and therefore the travel distance is not too far.

If you destroy another ship - no matter if human or NPC - that was not marked as "wanted", you won't only be fined: you get a bounty on your head and the so-called "notoriety" increases by the value "1".

(You can find your current notoriety value in the right in-ship window in the tab on the far left, next to "Balance" and "Rebuy Cost")

This bounty on your head (ship) leads to you being attacked by computer-generated bounty hunters and the occasional scan by law enforcement will result in an immediate attack.

In case you not only destroyed a „clean" NPC but a „clean" human player, your bounty will be increased even more: For each notoriety point you receive 10% of the difference between the insurance sums of your ship and your opponent's ship. This is meant to be a punishment for destroying smaller ships. In any case, your ship will get "hot" and you pay extra for any changes to modules or transport as long as your bounty is not paid.

The notoriety value is of great importance. Apart from adapting the „cost" of killing in terms of ever-increasing bounties for each increased notoriety, it generates an even more violent police reaction in case of „bad deeds" on your side – up to the appearance of ATR – advanced tactical response – which is a really devastating „special forces" group of police. Do not expect to survive more than 10 seconds with ATR's arrival.

Having notoriety does even more: You have to live with quite some restrictions until it is back to zero - and that takes a while: Two hours per notoriety point.

A value of 5 requires 10 (!) hours in the game to go back to zero (and possibly a final jump to another system, since it will only be updated then). As a result, the bad guys are even worse today than they used to be - according to the old saying „Now that my reputation is ruined I am free to do whatever I want" - and on the other hand, the casual gangsters are a lot braver today. A bad example of more punishment creating worse crimes.

In case you got notoriety, temporarily move to a nearby "anarchy" system, which is naturally more tolerant of criminals. After notoriety has faded away, you should visit an "Interstellar Factor", a place to pay fines and bounties „remotely". These are usually available at independent stations. Starport Services ? Contacts. Prepare to pay additional fees or cash in on bounties with a deduction from the proceeds – in return, you get a safe place that doesn't fire at you immediately because of your „wanted" station, which might happen at the place you „earned" your bounty.

5.4 Exploration

With version 3.3, the mechanics used until then in the area of exploration were revised and massively expanded.

It is no longer necessary to carry an "advanced" scanner, as it is now installed as standard in every ship („d-scanner"). However, it is important to check the key assignments before departure so that all necessary exploration equipment has been assigned to corresponding keys. Elite doesn't (always) do that by itself, at least not so reliably that you can be sure it all works when you need it to.

The „d-scanner" automatically does a "small" scan in every system you arrive at. That doesn't create much data or income, but those who jump a lot and further away can earn a decent extra income with not too much extra work involved:

Simply look into the "Universal Cartographics" when docking at the station and sell the collected data there.

By assigning the advanced scanner „d-scanner" or „discovery scanner" to an unused fire button (unused in supercruise) in the right in ship window's „fire groups" tab (standard key: "4") you can scan a whole system on a system level by simply keeping this fire button pressed until the „d-scanner" shows completion in the HUD. Completion is also marked with a „honk" tone, similar to an earth's ocean liner's fog horn.

If you're traveling in areas you haven't traveled before, scanning entire systems can earn you a lot of money. On longer distances, 50-100,000 credits per jump are possible without any further effort.

Of course, scanning the system structure is not everything. More interesting - especially from a financial point of view - is the detailed scanning of planetary objects. Some of them, for example, water worlds and Earth-like planets generate a huge income, with an additional bonus if they have not yet been scanned or/and mapped in detail by anyone before or/and if they are also suitable for terraforming. More about this in the "Path to Wealth".

In order to capture a planet in detail, you fly toward it until you look at it from a distance of about 0.10 light seconds (ls), then switch to the exploration mode (blue color, assign keys!) and activate the surface scanner. This then changes to a planet-only overview, which seems complicated at first, but quite functional with a bit of practice.

On this screen, you can see the currently available probes on the right-hand side of the frontal view. You can now send reconnaissance drones to the planet or its ring(s). The goal now is to capture the planet (and possibly its ring(s)) using these drones to cover 100% of the planet's surface (and placing a single shot on the ring of interest).

After firing a limpet at the (possibly existing) ring (note "ring" flashes visibly when aiming and being able to hit the ring), it has proved successful to first "deliver" a limpet to the planet's center.

After this central limpet, you now aim around the planet in steps of about 60 degrees (two-three spiked stars, one upright, one head down) and send one limpet each on the way to cover the side areas of the planet.

The last step is to look at how far you have to go to the outside until the display shows "Missed". Then you fire the drones just below this angle to let them fly to the back of the planet. So you use the gravitational pull of the planet to fire "around it."

The display at the bottom left will eventually show "100% coverage" - so the planet is not only captured but also mapped in detail. For this, you get the most money when you hand in the cartography data.

Be advised that surface scanning can hardly be told on theory alone, you might need some experience for hitting 100% in one go or for even reducing the number of probes/drones needed. It's a game (simulator) after all and with experience comes to rank, class, honor and ... just kidding.

Note: At the time of going to press, no reliable data on income from exploration after the 3.3 update is available. What is certain, however, is that the income has increased considerably once again and that even with regular exploration, an average of more than 100,000 credits per jump can certainly be achieved.

5.4.1 Path To Wealth [HOWTO]

Often described as „Road To Riches" this is a method to make lots of progress in a minimum of time

Learn tasks needed for Exploration
Make lots of money
Increase your Exploration rank

Of course, it is up to each "commander" to decide whether he wants to explore systems already discovered by others in order to gain income and a good exploration rank, but false moral aside, this procedure is simple and effective and should, therefore, be mentioned as an easy way for maximum (legal and honorable) progress:

The path to wealth (not „riches" as you only rake in 5-10 million per hour which is a wonderful way to make money for a beginner but not the way to go for „maximum greed" later on) consists of **three steps:**

1. Install the essential equipment:

It is more than helpful to create a ship setup that provides as much jump range as possible. A fuel scoop is absolutely mandatory and a surface scanner is needed for maximum income.

In principle, it doesn't matter what kind of ship you use - as long as it has enough jump range (every light year counts) and room for a surface scanner and a large fuel scoop. Thinking about these three factors is enough to create a viable setup.

For those who don't have much money, we recommend the "Hauler". Not really an appealing ship but as mommy always told you: Inner values count: The hauler is a reliable and well performing personal transporter on a budget. And with this strength in mind an unbeatable low budget exploration vessel - for less than 700,000 credits, fully equipped!

The procedure itself is simple:

Just buy a Hauler and remove all "optional" modules. Buy a "3B" fuel scoop, an additional "1C" fuel tank with 2 tons capacity and a detailed surface scanner. Remove the weapon and buy a heatsink launcher in one of the utility slots. Then change all core modules to "D" quality for less weight, each of them with the highest available size (number, for example, "4D", where the number should be as large as possible for the given slot).

This will result in an exploration ship that travels at least 28 light years per jump and performs at least 6 jumps with a total range of 200 light years without refueling (in case you forget). And this for less than 700,000 credits.

If you have more money available yet, you can equip a Diamondback Explorer for about 15 million credits according to the same scheme. Or an ASP Explorer for around 25 million. There are plenty of possibilities. (Did I mention that the Orca is also a great exploration ship for the bargain price of about 100 million credits?)

2. Travel from Earth-Like to Earth-Like

Visit a list of systems containing earth-like planets (and sometimes water worlds), which are each scanned and mapped in detail for maximum income and rank increase.

You can get this list on one of the many websites about "road to riches elite dangerous" - created according to your preferences. Just use the term in quotation marks in a search engine of your choice.

I don't add a (complete) list here, because the elite universe is changed every now and then. The list would thus be outdated and frustrating, and it is precisely these that this book wants to avoid.

I recommend instead to feed the search engine of your choice with the above search. This gives ample results with current data or generators that spit out suitable systems for you. If you don't wish to do so now or for a test run on this method, check the book's addendum for a short list of earth likes which are close to the bubble's center.

As soon as you got a list of target systems, the procedure is easy: You enter the target system into the galactic map, create a route and fly there (Settings: „Fastest" - not economical. No neutron star boost. No FSD boost).

On the way to your next target system, you simply „honk" scan each system you pass: after entering the system and while avoiding the main star(s), you press the assigned button for your d-scanner to get a rough scan of the systems you go through. This provides lots of additional income and exploration rank.

While „on the go", make sure to watch your fuel tank. Refill when at 50% or less. Fly safe!

Once in the target system, you make it a habit to fill the tank to 100% before turning away from the main star(s). While doing so, „honk" scan the system as you did with your waypoints. After scanning it, open your „system map" and take a look at it.

The planets concerned (earth likes and water worlds) are usually easily recognizable at first sight, if not just use the planet's description or designation in order to find out which one to target and to fly to.

Hint: Letters in description/designation of a planet tells you which main star is the start of the planet's row in the map. A is first, B is second, etc...

Numbers are telling you at which position you should take a look for the planet.

Planet A 4 would be the fourth position right of the first main star from the top.

Designations like AB describe the position between main star A and B. It's quite logical even for non-astronomy-buffs.

When near the designated planet – 0.10ls or less – scan it as described above until you see 100% of it mapped. This is your main source of income and rank.

Off you go to your next target system.

3. Cashing in

After visiting as many systems as possible you can cash in finally. Be advised that all collected cartography data is lost in case you die. Take care when approaching the station.

Please select a station to dock and open the starport services page once docked inside.

Using the starport services menu, look left at "Universal cartographics". There you can sell one page at a time (a button with the inscription "sale page" at the top). You will also be shown how much this page brings in.

Please note that only cartography data that has been obtained at least 20 light years away from your point of sale can be sold, the rest will be stored until you exceed this distance. This is not really of interest when doing „the procedure" to known systems, but could be later on.

This method of „going to known places" yields at least 6-10 million credits per hour. If you started with a Hauler, you should dock and collect after 3 hours at the latest. An ASP Explorer with more comfort, more agility in supercruise and greater jump range is waiting for you. The improved performance increases your payout and decreases your level of effort.

In the end, not only the money counts but also the acquired exploration rank. Even if you don't go as far as Elite Rank, you'll still get a higher ranking and therefore much better missions. If you don't bother doing this for a few days, you can even reach exploration elite rank and gain access to Shinrarta Dezhra. All ships, all modules at one place with a discount!

5.4.2 Real Exploration

Real exploration, i.e. without a list of given systems, is an art in itself.

For beginners, a small round trip to a place not more than 1000 light-years away is recommended - this manageable journey is settled in one evening without much homesickness and without much expenditure or threat.

Those who already dare to undock for longer journeys, should at least once make the trip to the center of our galaxy and visit Sagittarius A. The ones aiming for more social interaction can fly to Jaques, the android whose frame shift drive's malfunction has left him stranded 20.000 light years away from SOL in today's COLONIA, a kind of second civilization outside the "bubble".

On the subject of exploration, there will (hopefully soon) be an extra book or booklet containing details like repair drones, maintenance units, landings on high gravity planets, etc. For a pure beginner's book like this, that would simply go too far.

5.5 Mining

Mining was once the chill-out area of Elite Dangerous. Whoever knew that lucrative ore could also be found outside the pirate-infested resource zones - in peace and without any danger - flew once every now and then to an untouched planet ring of his choice for some relaxed and chilled mining. Arriving there, one, two or three Gin Tonic (underage? juice!) and filled his cargo area with Painite and other nice things.

The big point of criticism - and rightly so - was that it was simply nothing more than "relaxed shooting at rocks". Problem with that? As much as one can enjoy some relaxed „chill out phase" after some time mining became more than repetitive and really bothersome.

It's all different now. Or maybe not. Not so, because mining has gained much more depth, but also it is because you can choose what you want to do in mining. Improvement. Much.

Location, location, location!

Long before you search for "hot spots" at rings or scan these for possible mining locations, you must first be aware of this: The best „harvest" in mining is to be found in mostly deserted places as every other Cmdr diminishes the amount of lore at a location for a certain time.

For finding a less frequented system, just use an unpopulated one a bit further from the „main traffic areas" like SOL or Eravate. Going on a 100+ ly mining trip can increase your income and your satisfaction a lot.

For finding such places, use the galaxy map or even better (and way more convenient) use eddb.io. There you select "body" and search for "pristine" and "metallic" around the current location.

The resulting list offers either rings or belts. For simplicity choose a ring, in which it is easier to find one's way around. The ring always has a planet you can lock as a navigational target to orient yourself on. A belt is just a bunch of rocks.

The system's and the planet's designations are important, for example: "DELKAR 7 A" as a list result. Unfortunately, this list does not distinguish between the "A" planet (a sub-planet of the main planet it is orbiting around) and the "A" ring (the innermost of several rings or parts of one ring surrounding the planet).

So you have to be careful here because there is a risk of confusion:

In our example we are dealing with the Delkar system and Planet 7, but not with Planet "A" in the orbit of Planet 7, but with the so-called "A" ring. As already mentioned, this refers to the innermost part of the ring.

So if you look for a ring at "Delkar 7A" (the planet that orbits the planet Delkar 7), you won't find one, because the ring (its „A" part) surrounds Delkar 7. The correct - and better - name would be "Delkar 7 A-Ring" in contrast to Delkar 7 A (-Planet).

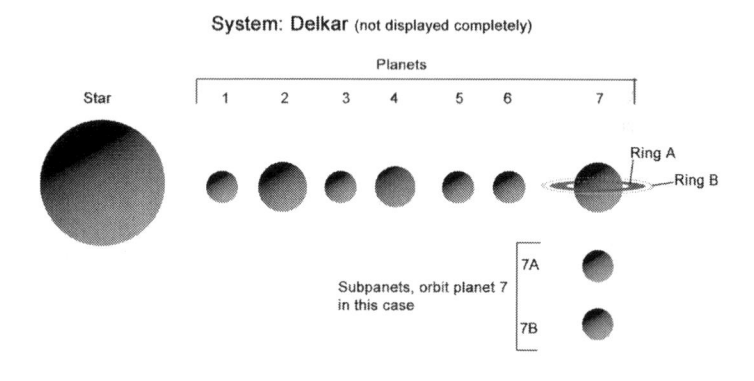

System: Delkar (not displayed completely)

Star — Planets 1 2 3 4 5 6 7 — Ring A, Ring B

Subpanets, orbit planet 7 in this case: 7A, 7B

The following descriptions depend on the ship size used and its possibilities - smallest ships like the sidewinder can only mine in a very limited and by no means lucrative way.

For real mining with all options, you need a ship with at least 5 weapon suspensions and enough optional module slots. The ASP Explorer (approx. 20 million credits) or the T-6 Transporter (only 4 hardpoints! - approx. 10 million credits) are the cheapest ships for this purpose.

5.5.1 Basic Mining With A Very Small Ship

Mining below the "Cobra Mk3" class

If you are still flying a sidewinder (or another ship with a similarly small number of weapons and module slots), you should keep your hands off mining: Too much effort for a measly payout. If you wish to try it anyway, here are some tips:

Minimum mining equipment for the smallest ships (Sidewinder, Hauler, Eagle)

1. A mining laser

Please note: this laser is not suitable for combat and its range is very limited. It also drains a lot of power from the power distributor, so please use "4 pips in WEP" before and while shooting at rocks, otherwise, fire duration will be quite short.

2.) A refinery

This module converts several fragments collected (and previously detached from the asteroid) into one marketable ton of cargo each.

3.) As much cargo space as possible
You should leave the cargo hold empty if you don't have a limpet controller with you. It is then gradually filled by the refinery with processed material.

The smallest ships like the sidewinder don't use limpets as there won't be cargo space left if they do...

... in addition, they can only harvest asteroid fragments by shooting chunks off of them. Surface mining is an option, but the lack of hardpoints makes regular mining less profitable. Deep core mining is impossible due to the lack of a class 2 weapon hardpoint.

Using a small ship, use mining zones near you as the fuel scoop needed for reaching mining areas in 100+ light years of distance further reduces your options in terms of mining equipment or cargo space.

The game update in Q1/2019 has brought additional optional module slots, so it is possible to „go places" in a mining equipped sidewinder. It is of no use, though: you better use these new small slots for additional cargo or a small collector limpet controller.

Once dropped in the mining area of your choice – preferably some resource zone near a metallic rich and a not depleted planet, please make it a habit to „clean your radar".
When you drop at a resource zone, you are not in danger of being attacked: You got no cargo or just a few limpets. You are not wanted. In short: Pirates consider you boring.

This changes when you start collecting valuable stuff. So, first of all, make sure you got zero ships on your radar. Blinking radar symbols are ships that are out of your radar range. Your radar range. Not theirs. Get rid of them. Fly straight on along the asteroid belt until you are on your own. Do not start mining before you are sure of being alone.

If you are "safe", you simply shoot at an asteroid with your mining (regular mining laser, not an abrasive one) laser.
You can then check if it's full of valuable ore or just useless stuff by targetting the fragments you have chipped just off of it. Standard key "T".

Mining with the smallest ships is only worthwhile - if at all - if you have accepted a mining mission that promises high returns with the smallest quantities. This is very rare and your effort and time invested are usually below the hourly income that can be achieved with other activities.

5.5.2 Advanced Mining With A Decent Income

The minimum equipment for effective fragment mining (for deep core mining hop to the next subchapter, please):

1.) A small or medium-sized ship with proper weapons and cargo hold, the smallest ship suitable for this purpose is the Cobra Mk III (or a Viper Mk IV).

2.) A pulse wave analyzer (utility slot module) that scans the area in front of you and highlights „promising" asteroids when near.

3.) At least two mining lasers. This statement is somewhat general as it is based on personal preferences, the power distributor size of the chosen ship and some other factors. You should use at least two size 1 mining lasers - or at least one size 2 mining laser. Do yourself a favor and take two or more, otherwise, you'll shoot at rocks for a long time until they're depleted as in „fully harvested".

4.) Depending on how many weapon slots you have and how much energy your ship can provide from the power plant, you might want to use a mining laser, a subsurface displacement missile and a seismic charge launcher with you, although the seismic charge launcher really is for deep core mining – next subchapter.

5.) The refinery - of course – is the heart of the whole task. Materials collected by the limpets are converted into cargo by the refinery as described above.

6.) A prospector limpet controller of at least class 1 is necessary to comfortably investigate targeted asteroids.

> **Note:** Class 1A is preferable to "cheaper classes" due to the higher range. Larger classes (3 is the next larger) have the advantage that you can have two prospector drones active at the same time, but this requires some practice and adaptation, usually, class 1 is enough.

7.) At least one Class 3 collection limpet controller.

The more collection limpets you can send out at one time, the more efficient your refinery, although when saturated with a high number of limpets delivering fragments, even the biggest refinery will form a queue of limpets at the cargo hatch. Rule of thumb: Twice as many limpets as your refinery's size class e.g. a 2A refinery runs fine with 4 active limpets.

There's a fine balance between the number of limpets, the number of mining lasers, the model of your power distributor and the size of your refinery with no „one size fits all" formula for this. Become a miner and „feel" the need for equipment...

8.) A detailed surface scanner to look for special areas („hot spots") at the beginning of the mining process (i.e. still approaching the ring).

This more targeted search for valuable ore begins before the actual approach to the rings of a planet. When about 1-2 light seconds away from the planet or its rings, reduce speed to a complete standstill (standard key "X" for 0% thrust) and scan the system with the built-in detailed exploration scanner (d-scanner), which is standard in all ships. The default key for this is "M" - but this "default" is not safe, in case of doubt please look at your key assignments in the main menu's options.

When the ship's scan mode (FSS) opens, you are asked to do an initial scan using "Insert" (the key above the arrow key block).

When this initial scan is complete, please leave the scan menu in order to activate the surface scanner in the next step. This optional section module should have been installed and assigned to a fire button that is not used for anything else. If in doubt, please open a new fire group (a vertical column) without any other functions for less interference. You don't want to have to check your assignments all the time.

The surface scanner shows a cockpit-less image of the planet in front of you. First, you aim at a ring and trigger a surface scanner probe using the right mouse button (or fire 2 or whatever you assigned).

> **Tip:**
> As said before, it is important to take into account that all masses in space create gravity and therefore „bend" a projectile's trajectory. So it makes more sense to aim at the outermost areas of the ring and check if you see the message „ring" when firing your probe. This ensures that you hit the ring in any case and that the probe is not distracted by the gravitational pull of the planet.

If using the probe successfully, the ring of the planet will light up briefly and you can return to the normal view.

In normal view, any existing "hot spots" in the normal field of view should now be visible as golden, brightly shining, more or less circular surfaces. In the left in-ship-window (default key: "1") use the navigation tab short list to see all hot spots listed. None there? None in the ring. Check another ringed planet then.

The – hopefully found - hot spots do not mean that the given material is to be found only there exclusively, but that this material occurs in some statistical accumulation there (As in „mostly the stuff that gave the name to the hotspot, but there might be other stuff, too").

You will find low-temperature diamonds in a void opal hot spot now and then and the other way round. This is valid for all valuable ore that is found in a ring of that type (Icy/Rocky/Metallic differentiate more or less clearly in regard to the presence of certain ore). It's just: Search for „A", then go „A" not for anything else, wondering why you don't find „A" in a „B" spot.

In the beginning, it makes the most sense to choose a "Painite" hot spot (pristine and metallic rings), because this high-priced material can be found without problems. If you have some experience with this, you can choose to go for even more expensive materials at their hot spots.

FYI: A hot spot, unlike "real" navigation points and mining areas, is simply approached by „crashing" into it: You slowly fly towards the hot spot using "4 in SYS" for maximum shield strength and simply „collide" with the planetary ring at its location. No fear, your ship will survive the mishap with minuscule damage.

Arriving at the "ring" in normal speed mode (no „c" (speed of light) or „km/s" on your speed display), the "pulse wave analyzer" is now used to "tap" the asteroids for abnormalities. Yellow, red and black discolorations indicate worthwhile ore deposits – even when shown as a grid.

Now you set course for such a "colorful" asteroid and fire a prospector limpet at it.

> **Important**
> Limpets are slow, their maximum single-target speed is only 200 m/s. Make sure you fly slower than that when sending a (prospector) limpet. Flying faster than the limpet often results in a crash, destroying the limpet.

Shortly after firing the prospector limpet at the asteroid, please use the "target ahead" function (standard key: "T") on it for tracking and later on for receiving prospector information. After reaching the asteroid, this limpet shows its analysis on the left side of the information window.

The hardest part is identifying materials that really pay off. Open eddb.io's commodity price list in a browser window or print it out once for a short view on what's worth of being mined and what is not.

Furthermore, it is your decision where you draw the line to "worth it or not". You can "aim for mass mining" and just collect anything that delivers more than 2000 credits per ton, or be picky and just collect the expensive ore.

5.5.3 Deep Core Mining

Even if I normally reject telling people about „the only way to do something right", there is indeed often a "maximum" of efficiency, a more or less ideal way. Even if there are usually several ways leading to what one's aiming for, there often is a way to reach a set goal with a minimum of equipment and effort.

In order to take advantage of all the opportunities that mining in Elite Dangerous offers, you - unfortunately – need a slightly larger ship.

The good - and at the same time bad - news: the smallest and cheapest ship that can be considered is an ASP Explorer with a total cost of at least 20 million credits. (Good as it's not a 500+ million Anaconda, bad as you might not have earned these 20 million credits yet).

> **Pro tip:** Elite Dangerous has a large number of polite, generous and helpful „players". Do not hesitate to ask higher ranked CMDRs for help or even for funds. You can be assisted in making progress with news, information, tips, assistance in combat or trade. Even sharing a completed wing mission is possible. Ask. Most won't bite :-)

Deep Core Mining – or advanced mining for maximum income – makes use of a lot of the basics talked about before. In addition to refineries and limpets for prospecting asteroids and limpets for collecting materials, you can purchase at least 2 mining lasers. It is important to pay attention to a surface scanner, a pulse wave analyzer and the special weapons: An abrasion blaster, a rocket launcher for subsurface displacement missiles and a seismic loader.

The first part of the procedure is about the same as described in the subchapter before, up to the scanning of the possible asteroids in the ring using the pulse wave scanner. The difference is that with full equipment you can also operate the whole range of ore extraction and therefore you switch your main focus on finding deep core deposits of the most lucrative kind, like void opals.

If, for example, one sees superficial deposits of valuable material, these are simply removed with the abrasion laser. In contrast to the regular fragments, which are mined with the mining laser, the yield here is significantly higher. A single fragment results in a whole ton of cargo and is usually of higher value than fragmented (chipped off using a regular mining laser) ore.

Even more interesting, although not more lucrative, are subsurface deposits of valuable materials. These are removed by positioning oneself directly above the materials in question and launching an unguided subsurface displacement missile from a distance of around 400-800m. Keep the fire button pressed and pay attention to the appearing "treadmill". In this, there are blue areas that represent the layer in which valuable material can be expected.

If you release the fire button at the right moment when the pointer points to a blue surface, a detonation in this layer is triggered... and you made it.

The most lucrative method, but also the most complicated, is blowing up an asteroid with deep core deposits using a perfectly dosed amount of explosives, not too little, not too much of it. However, if the core contains one of the rare (exotic sounding) materials or even void opals, this is extremely worthwhile. Void Opals, for example, can be sold for up to 1.6 million credits per ton. A single asteroid yields 10-15 tons. Do the math.

When handling an asteroid containing valuable deep core ore (check his color: It looks „pee" yellow, usually without a „grid" and rarely with red or black nuances), you first check for fissures (cracks) being visible while approaching it. Using night vision makes this much easier.

You then place seismic charges at fissures until reaching optimal yield as displayed in the top right corner of your forward view. Instead of using a low yield charge on a low yield fissure, a medium yield charge on a medium fissure and a high yield charge on a – surprise – high yield fissure, there's a way to make things more efficient:

Simply place maximum (high) yield charges on the first 2-3 fissures you target, no matter what kind of intensity is shown when targetting them. When approaching the optimal yield level in the top right diagram, adjust by using the yield you think is optimal on the next fissure you „treat". This might create a problem in placing too much total yield in your first few attempts. After a few asteroids, it becomes a 100% working procedure and will save you 1-3 seismic charges per detonation.

When in doubt, prefer overcharging over placing not enough charges. Your harvest will be reduced by „overblowing" your asteroid, by placing too-small-a-yield there's no harvest at all.

The explosives you set are fixed at 120 seconds, i.e. 120 seconds after the first charge has been applied. In the "contacts" area in your left in-ship-window, you can reduce this countdown delay to near-instant detonation once having placed all needed yields.

You can also defuse the explosive charges – one by one – which can be helpful to adjust yield. The latter may make sense if one of the charges has chosen an explosive force that is too high and/or the message appears that the total explosive force is too high.

Two factors are important during and after blasting: On the one hand, you should not be surprised if the ship placed too close to the blasting takes damage or is even destroyed. Distance helps, one kilometer is usually enough.

On the other hand, blasting generates dust. A lot of it. This obstructs your own view. It is therefore really advisable to switch to night vision if you haven't yet. You can find the assigned key in the section Options > Key assignment.

5.6 Collecting Cargo In Space

Please do yourself a favor and complete the tutorials. This advice was given earlier on, but it's more than important to do so when doing things like collecting cargo or other stuff in open space. It's just helpful having done everything in the tutorials at least once.

Collecting (legal and illegal goods), rescue capsules and (later) materials for the engineers is something that you will usually have limpets do for you later on, but sometimes you will just not have some of these with you (as you need cargo space and a collector limpet controller, for which there simply is not enough space in your ship at times)

By learning to collect items from space manually, you avoid the frustration of facing something you desperately need floating near you – then destroying it out of incompetence instead of successfully collecting it.

(The use of the collective limpet controller and its drones/limpets is described in more detail both in the mining chapter and in the module area).

To collect cargo in space, please first retract your weapons and landing gear. Both can be blocking the „flow" to the cargo scoop, kicking your desired objects into space.

After that, please deploy your cargo scoop (Standard key "HOME").

> **CAUTION** With most keyboards, the key for jettisoning all cargo on board is 'end', directly adjacent below the 'home' key. You would not be the first CMDR in Elite losing all his cargo by hitting the wrong button.

If the key has been reassigned or you are using a HOTAS or game controller, please open the right in-ship-window (default key "4"), select "ship" (top left tab) and use the function to extend the cargo scoop.

With the cargo scoop extended, you must now select the object of desire as your target. The default key "G" for "Cycle Targets" will not work for floating objects shown in light grey on the radar screen. You have to place the object in the middle of your windscreen and then use "Target Ahead" (default key "T").

Once activated, you'll see a small additional 80s-arcade-style screen to the left of the radar. This little tool from now on is all you should be interested in: In order to collect freight, you have to "collide" slowly with the item from your cargo scoop's point of view – which is represented by the little additional screen. By using your windscreen's view, you will miss a lot as – depending on your ship's size and your cockpit's position – you are quite a bit higher in position than your cargo scoop is. Centering your 'object of desire' in your windscreen means missing it big time with your cargo scoop.

Now fly towards the target object at a speed of 20-40 m/s and keep it centered in the small "80s screen".
If you should miss the object despite your enormous abilities as a space pilot, then please do not chase after it. Stop (standard key "X"), then go a few meters into reverse (standard key "S") and then start another attempt from 50-150 meters distance.

Please keep in mind that every unsuccessful ramming does more damage to the object than waiting for something to calm the accelerated object down again and you can pick it up in peace.

Cargo is vulnerable. It slowly degrades until destruction. More problematic is damage done by ramming it. Be careful.

5.7 Wealth For The Impatient

Money rules the world, and if you're aiming for anything bigger than a Cobra Mk 3 you should consider earning a lot of it.

Although – or even because – Elite is not a classical MMO game with a defined endgame, but more a vast space simulator, you should not grind for money.

Work-life-balance is everything – keep an eye on yourself if your goals are set reasonably and if you're starting to burn out. Immersion is often strong and some people tend to exhaust themselves when grinding for goals.

If you're one of the more money-oriented commanders, though, here is the - present - way to go for maximum income.
(Note: You will find more ways to 'mo' money' googling terms around it. When doing so, check their date. Some kind of income has been nerfed, others have been improved. For small ships, rare good trading can be a viable (and fun) option, these days. Just as an example.)

Phase 1: Sidewinder (No money earned yet)

Completely out of funds and with only a small set of skills in a tiny ship.. you're doomed.

More seriously, you got options for earning money, but they're quite limited to what you will experience later on.

Maximum income in this phase is achieved through two options:
When meeting more experienced and higher ranked commanders, simply ask them if they would help you out a bit. This can be done by sharing (already fulfilled) wing mission contracts with high payouts like wing assassinations or „bring in commodities" missions. If you or your new high ranked buddy are not into free giveaways, you can accompany him while 'harvesting' bounties in resource zones. Just talk, a 'big brother' is a good thing in a 'cutthroat galaxy'.

Just... be careful when people try to actively recruit you into groups (squadrons) – these are often not the same from the inside as promoted on the outside...

Since the starter system was moved away from LHS 3447 / Eravate / Kremainn / LTT 15574's area, it's harder to meet people. If you don't meet higher ranked commanders, simply use the discord chat described in the 'socializing' chapter. Ask and you will be given.
Apart from the classical MMO way of doing 'quests' which are called missions in Elite – which does create a good income but can be tiresome and boring, you should consider earning some money by 'harvesting' bounties using law enforcement. Described in here in depth, you basically join a group of 'cops' and start firing at a wanted fugitive until his ship explodes, cashing in on the bounty while letting do the cops most of the work. This not only ranks you up a bit in combat and teaches you the basics of fighting in Elite Dangerous, but it also lets you move to Phase 2 in less than an hour.

Phase 2: Hauler (more than ca. 1 million in assets)

Once you have earned the "first million", you can move on to "forced exploration" – visiting systems with known valuable objects like Earth-like planets or water worlds.

- Buy a cheap Hauler
- Get rid of all optional modules
- Get the best Frame Shift Drive "Largest Number & Quality A"
- All other modules on "Largest Number & Quality D"
- Install Fuel Scoop "3B"

https://www.spansh.co.uk/riches

Then simply go to the website above and create a route where you can "scan" at least 300,000 credits (or 600,000 credits for the greedy) per destination and follow the instructions for the "Path to Wealth" in the exploration section of this book. (The first 50 systems of such a route can be found in the annex. Going for these 50 systems (5-10 hours of time needed) you will earn at least 50 million credits plus lots of exploration rank for better missions)

„Forced exploration" In this way you earn 6-10 million credits per hour, which means that you can move to phase 3 after a maximum of 5 hours (or 30 systems).

Phase 3: ASP Explorer (more than ca. 30 million in assets)

With more than 30 million in assets, you can go for 'core mining'. You don't have to use a 25+ million ASP Explorer, but it is the minimum equipment to fully utilize this mining method in terms of money earned per time unit.

You can use a ca. 5 million Cobra Mk3 for deep core mining, but you will have to return to a point of sale after one harvested asteroid. If you use a Cobra, switch to an Asp Explorer as soon as possible.

How "Deep Core Mining" is carried out is described in detail in the "Mining" chapter. Those who have no luck in choosing the right asteroids are recommended to search the internet for a few pictures of typical "Elite Dangerous void opal asteroids" with the help of a search engine. Alternatively, you can politely ask someone for help on a first tour in the Discord listed under Social. Elite has a very helpful and friendly "community".

(Printed pictures of asteroids are of not much use: colors and shapes are looking quite differently on e-readers and even more so on paper)

6. Ships – Shipyard And Outfitting

In the four years that I have been introducing new "commanders" to Elite Dangerous (and sometimes accompanied them longer), I have been asked again and again what is the most important thing I have to say about "ships and their equipment".

The answer, each time: "Ships are only the basis, the choice of modules and weapons is everything".

Of course, this has to be enjoyed with a pinch of salt, but it is a very important base rule: There are excellent combat ships based on ship types that are at best "allrounders": Asp Explorer, Python, Krait Mk II, Anaconda. You should be aware that many of the options in terms of building your dream ship in Elite Dangerous are only available by using the Engineers in the Horizons package.

Nevertheless, even without horizons and engineers, there are many possibilities to customize ships and even without an Engineer performance upgrade, Elite's ships are capable of taking on the strongest computer opponents.

6.1 Buying Ships But Buying Them Right

Before you buy a new ship, you should have a rough idea of what this ship should do for you.

You should definitely use a ship configurator like coriolis.io (CORIOLIS.IO), because it saves a lot of effort and hassle doing a 'dry run' in configuring your ship and having all performance data at one glimpse instead of creating a 'real life' build of a ship for hours just to realize it's not living up to its promises.

You can use the data given in outfitting, but not only is the information there less readable and less verbose, you need to pay for modules and fly around for availability first – let alone doing all the engineering if using Horizons.

When building a ship, it cannot be stressed often that there's a 5% deductible ('rebuy sum') in case of seeing your ship destroyed, which is of course much more significant if a ship cost 300 million instead of 15 million.

A 'wise commander' uses the smallest ship needed for a certain task and keeps an eye on outfitting cost, especially with larger ships. Quite often the cheaper version of a ship is the better and more viable one.

(Example: Using a Cobra Mk3 and having the urgent wish to strengthen your hull's defensive capabilities, you can either buy a military bulkhead instead of a light one, or you can opt for a 2D hull reinforcement package. The bulkhead needs ca. 340.000 credits in funds, the hull reinforcement package needs ca. 36.000 credits in funds. This is about 300.000 credits more in your account and with that about 15.000 credits less to pay in case of a destroyed ship. The 25 (!) tons less in weight which make the difference of an agile, joyous ship and a small moon set aside – 25 tons is about 10% of the total weight of a Cobra Mk3...)

Some stations or even entire systems offer special features for buying a ship:

The 'shopping paradise' Jameson Orbital in the Shinrarta Dezhra system (maximum availability on everything: all ships, all modules with a discount of 5% on it) is unfortunately only accessible with an elite rank in exploration, trade or combat. ELIT'ism at its finest, sorry.

Another 'full stock' shopping center is the ground station I Sola Prospect in the Brestla system. Horizon's owners can count on full availability here the same way as in Shinrarta Dezhra but in contrast to Shinrarta with a surcharge of 20%.

There are other stations with discounts on individual ships or modules, but the most interesting offer is that of Li-Yong Rui. This "Powerplay" character doesn't have a wider selection of ships than others, but they are - just like modules - generally offered with a 15% discount!

In order to benefit from this offer, one must specifically look for a system controlled by Li-Yong Rui (this status is important). The best way to do this is to use eddb.io / EDDB.IO, respectively its station database. Simply enter your current location, add power effect 'control' and power 'Li-Yong Rui'. The result is a list of stations under control of Li-Yong Rui. For the availability of your desired module(s), enter your demand in 'Station sells Modules'.

6.2 Modules

The choice of Modules are the one factor that makes a ship something special.

Far too many commanders choose modules following some "more cost = better choice" set of rules or by thinking about some 'more damage' or 'more defense' rule. It's not that simple.

In general, modules are named according to size and distinguishable quality, not according to size and "better" or "worse".

For regular modules (i.e. non-utility-section modules) the size is given in numbers from 1 to 8. The larger the number, the larger the module.

In general, you should always use the largest module that fits into the existing module slot. This is all the more important for mass-relevant modules such as the jump drive – with an FSD a number too small your ship will have an extremely short range, although using 'best performance' quality: If, for example, a ship has a maximum "4" shaft here, changing from a class "4A" drive to a "3A" drive can quickly reduce the available jump range from 25 light years to 6 light years. In this way, you may unintentionally end up with a useless ship.

The modules' qualities are described in letters ranging from "A" to "E", where E is the cheapest variant and A the most expensive variant. Although A has the best performance without exception, it's not only the most costly but also the most power hungry in terms of drawing energy from the power plant (and sometimes also from the power distributor). In addition, variant A can also mean a lot more weight, which is a very important factor.

The one-word-mnemonics like 'Economy' I present in the following overview are a reminder for you, which should make it easier for you to know at first sight which main characteristics the modules have. That English terms are more practical from time to time may be forgiven, but so much English anyone can speak, even if he or she plays Elite in German.

E - Economy – Default module
- Lowest costs
- Weakest performance
- Medium to high weight
- Low energy consumption
- PLEASE DO NOT USE!

D - Diet – Minimum weight
- Favorable costs

- Enough power for most purposes
- Lowest weight
- Low energy draw, marginally more than "E
- USE PLENTY!

C - Compromise - For the undecided
- Moderate cost
- Moderate performance
- Moderate weight
- Moderate energy consumption
- USE IF 'A' IS TOO COSTLY OR TOO POWER HUNGRY!

B - Bullshit - Way too heavy

- On average 1/3 of the cost of 'A'.
- More power than C
- Maximum weight
- High energy consumption
- DO NOT USE EVER!

A single 'B' module can raise your ship's weight unnecessarily. A perfect way to ruin a build.

A - A-Level - Maximum performance
- Most expensive module quality
- Best performance
- Weight at 'C' level
- Highest energy consumption in power plants and power distributors
- USE FOR MODULES YOU DESPERATELY NEED TO SEE PERFORMING ON HIGHEST LEVELS.

The three module categories explained in the following sometimes differ significantly from each other. Of course in the possibility of selection, but also in other important conditions and restrictions.

The subdivision of module types into compulsory modules and optional modules gives an approximate idea of what is of essential importance and what is not. Added to these sections comes are the no less important utility slots.

Using all potential in outfitting ships with certain modules, you can create ships with a maximum of agility by keeping weight extremely low, for example. This can be taken to extremes by using the Horizons package to further improve module performance and weight, resulting in ins ships capable of speeds in excess of 800 m/s that are actually combat ready.
Other examples are ships with enormously low heat generation, which can crawl for long periods of time, while thrusters and weapons are fully capable, upgraded in their hull strength to an extent that increases the stability of a Cobra Mk3, for example, to 15-20 times the normal. And all this only by some engineering work and "smart" changes to the equipment.

6.2.1 Internal Modules / Compulsory Modules

The internal modules are the least freely configurable ship modules.

Their size is usually a given. In addition to the maximum possible size of a module in a current module slot, which corresponds to the actual dimensions of the module slot, one or two numbers "smaller" are most often possible but often not feasible due to performance issues. In contrast to the optional modules, it is neither possible to omit an internal module as in keeping it empty and not using its determined function, nor to select it freely in any size of choice.

Their qualities do not differ from those of other modules such as those in the optional area. The classification according to chapter 6.2 "Modules" is to be applied here without restrictions.

The following list is not arranged according to the importance of the modules but follows their listing in the outfitting section when docked at a station.

6.2.1.1 Bulkheads

These modules are one of the ways to increase hull strength and resistance to certain types of damage. The basic value describes the protection against "raw" damage quality, such as being rammed or colliding with objects. Weapons such as the plasma accelerator and the rail gun are also predominantly aimed at raw damage, they deliver around 80% of their damage done in this damage quality.

If you "only" want to gain a little more security by reinforcing the shell a little, you should definitely ask yourself whether you really want to achieve this through alloys.

Not only are bulkheads extremely expensive, but they also come with a lot of surplus weight. A „military alloy" bulkhead reinforcement not only costs around 340.000 credits, but it also comes with 27 tons of additional weight, providing ca. 204 MJ of additional protection.

Using a simple hull reinforcement module instead, even a small one in class 2D drains your bank account only by around 36.000 credits.

You receive 190 MJ of additional hull protection – nearly the same amount of the bulkhead – and save about 25 tons of weight (!) as the little protection module only ways 2 tons.

So by sacrificing a class 2 module slot and filling it with a hull reinforcement module instead of choosing a prestigious huge bulkhead, you save about 90% of expenditures and more than 90% of the weight.
Like in ancient earth's atmospheric aviation, weight is a major factor in performance. In Elite, it's mostly about combat agility, but jump range is a huge factor, too. Not using strong bulkheads lowers your ship's weight by up to 10% or more. Think about the implications for your ship's performance!

For most ships 1-2 smaller hull reinforcements in the optional range are sufficient. Larger amounts of "Hull Reserve" are only common if you want to equip special types of ships, for example, 'silent runner' ships, or if you go hunting Thargoids. Both are much too complex to describe in detail in the beginner's area, so here in brief:

Bulkheads (Alloys)

Lightweight Alloys
- Little protection
- No additional cost

- No additional weight
- Great for ships that need to be extra light and rarely lose shields.

Reinforced Alloys
- Around 50% more protection
- Low additional cost
- Low additional weight
- Compromise for the undecided. Consider using a hull reinforcement package instead.

Military Grade Alloys
- Around 100% more protection
- High additional cost
- High additional weight
- Only use if you can't live without the extra protection. The weight is barely tolerable.

Light alloys, reinforced alloys, and military composite alloys provide protection against the various types of damage weighted as normal.

Their "raw" defense value is valid against thermal weapons (laser) without deduction, although they are somewhat weaker than the promised "raw" defense value against kinetic weapons (cannons of all kinds, approx. 10-15% deduction) and lose somewhat more against explosive weapons (missiles, torpedoes, approx. 25-30% deduction).

If you already know in advance that you will be facing a certain type of weapon in combat, it can be useful to choose one of the two specialized alloy types. For everyday use, there is neither the necessity nor a real sense for this since specialization can also be expected to have disadvantages.

Mirrored Surface Composite
About 100% more protection in "raw" defense value (analogous to "military composite")
Extremely expensive (more than twice as expensive as "military composite")
High additional weight (roughly analogous to "military composite")
Only a good thing if you know your enemy will mostly use thermal damage weapons (lasers) against your hull.

The mirrored version optimized against thermal weapons offers approximately 80% more protection against attacks with lasers, but only circa 50% protection of the "military composite" against kinetic weapons with approximately the same protection against explosive weapons.

So you really have to be sure that you are competing against an opponent without kinetic weapons, otherwise, this expensive gadget is a disadvantage! Choose wisely and prefer all-round solutions over special builds if in doubt.

Reactive Surface Composite
- About 100% more protection in "raw" defense value (analogous to "military composite")
- Extremely expensive (even more expensive than mirrored alloys!)
- High additional weight (analogous to "military composite")

- Only useful if you know in advance your enemy will do most of his damage on you using explosive (torpedoes, missiles) and kinetic (guns of all kind) weapons.

The reactive version optimized against explosive and kinetic weapons offers more protection against kinetic weapons (approx. 50%) and against explosive weapons (approx. 45%), but also slightly less protection against lasers (approx. 25%).

If it has to be something special and the disadvantages such as cost and weight (and deduction in some areas) are not important, the reactive surface is preferable to the mirrored surface, especially for faster ships.

The reason for this advice is the very small range of lasers, which lose their effect starting after 500-600 meters of distance and which are actually only a nice light show once being further away than 1500-2000 meters. A protective effect, especially against kinetic and explosive weapons with sometimes significantly greater range, is therefore generally the better choice. If you want to live with the cost and the weight.

6.2.1.2. Power Plant

The power plant is – who would have thought - one of the most important parts of a ship. Not only does it have to provide enough energy to supply all installed (and marked active) systems, it also contributes enormously to the ship's heat balance.

Unmodified smaller ships with energy-efficient and "cool" running weapons such as multi cannons and (small) burst or pulse lasers do not create enough heat to run into trouble.

Big ships or even smaller ships using weapons like rail guns or plasma accelerators, especially if modified for more offensive power can create enormous amounts of heat which has to be dissipated by ship mass. Some ships are generally cooler than others due to their overall mass and setup.

The amount of heat generated by the power plant is an important factor, as its efficiency coefficent is of great help when trying to avoid a constantly overheating ship build, even if one is building an exploration vessel or a space truck.
Therefore, it is not only important for power plants to deliver enough 'juice' to serve all modules installed (please check the module area on the right of the ship (standard key: "4")), but also to be of the least heat producing kind possible.

Selecting the right power plant is based on these criteria: First you choose the power plant that provides you with the necessary amount of energy. Then you check if you can install a small (number) power plant with the quality "A" doing the job. "A" is the most expensive, but not heavier than "C" and above all: The coolest.

Example:
Some Cobra Mk3 has an energy requirement of just under 12 MW (megawatt) and offers a class 4 module slot for the power plant. The suitable power plant in size 4 would be a "4C" - it offers 13 MW of energy, weighs 5 tons, costs about 160,000 credits and has an efficiency of 0.50.

If you now have some money available and continue looking around, you can choose a "3A" power plant instead - one number smaller and with an "A" rating. This costs 480,000 credits, around 3 times as much, but is 2.5 tons lighter and has an efficiency of 0.40 – which not only enhances your ship's agility by reducing weight, it generates about 1.2 'units' less heat per second – which is basically as much as a class 2 multi cannon!

Power produced x efficiency = heat per second
12 MJ x 0.5 = 6
12 MJ x 0.4 = 4.8
Difference: 1.2 units

The more energy to produce the more important the choice of the installed power plant. Bigger ships use 40+ MJ of heat, which results in enormous amounts of heat generated.
The slightly lower integrity due to the power plant's smaller size does not represent a significant factor, with the exception of very long exploration trips (100,000 light years and more!) or 'unprotected' combat in shieldless hull monsters.
In real operation, a beginner will probably not notice the 2.5 ton difference in weight any more than he will notice the 0.2 light-years increase in single jump range, but he will notice the temperature difference in dire situations as after accidentally dropping 'into' a main star. Overheating is way more benign in that case.

If you refuel at a star, the power plant generally generates 20% less heat per MW generated. This is noticeable in significantly lower temperatures and allows you to fly closer to the star. The shorter distance to the star is accompanied by increased refuelling speed. The refuelling process becomes faster and more relaxed.

Generally "A" power plants are the means of choice, so please only use "C" or "D" if a smaller "A" is not an alternative. And please, please, please (did I already say please?) keep your hands off "B" power plants (B = 'bullshit', remember?)! In the above example of a Cobra MK 3, this would result in an additional weight of 8 tons to the above 2.5 tonnes of an 'A' rated power plant. This is around 3% of the ship's total mass – you will feel this in flight and in terms of jump range, which will reduced by about half a light year.

6.2.1.3 Thrusters

Thrusters are not only important in combat applications. When undersized, handling in normal speed range becomes a pain and impair safety by seemingly endless braking distances or by drifting when doing turns. Try to hit a station's mail slot once while in a hurry using undersized thrusters. You won't forget that day. In fights, undersized thrusters kill off most of your ship's agility and reduce both, your time-on-target as your-time-in-a-safe-space.

Example: A Cobra Mk 3 equipped with thrusters of size '4A' (maximum size possible) has a top speed of 440 m/s or more when using boosters (depending on weight). It has a rotation rate of up to 45 degrees pitch (nose up/down) per second.

A Cobra Mk3 equipped with the "4E" standard thruster module is comparably overweight: a maximum of 400 m/s with a low ship weight (usually 380 m/s or even less in normal weight configurations) - and a maximum pitch rate of 40 degrees (usually significantly less) are the result.

The difference of ca. 60 m/s in speed and 5 degrees in pitch doesn't sound a lot, but consider running away from a 380 m/s enemy or trying to fight a ship with more pitch than you have.

In addition, agility is fun. And you don't want to miss out on the fun in your shiny space ship, do you?!
When making your choice of thrusters, you should always use the largest size (number!) that can be installed in your ship.

For some explorers it can make sense to use smaller thrusters. Especially if they are not planning to land on planets using the Horizons package (Try to arrest sink rate on a high gravity planet using weak thrusters, then live to tell the tale).

As described above, 'A' is the means of choice, never "B" (weight!). Whoever does not have the financial means nor the money for 'A', chooses 'C' for slightly more power than 'D' - or the latter for the lowest weight.

6.2.1.4. Frame Shift Drive FSD

The frame shift drive is responsible for travelling in supercruise mode (between planets – inside a system) and hyper-jumping into other systems.

The size and quality of the FSD make no difference to its behaviour in supercruise, but it does make a difference when jumping into other systems: Here the drives differ enormously in the achievable jump range.

The FSD should always and without exception be used in the largest class (number) possible. Smaller classes are usually not sufficient to even leave the current system, let alone travel further because of a lack of supported ship mass.

The quality of the FSD determines not only the range but also the heat generation during charging the drive for a jump. "E" qualities can cause damage to a ship by overheating every time it jumps, with otherwise usable design. Therefore FSD modules should not be used in that quality. Everything from 'D' to 'A' is fine, depending on your personal need for range.

> **Tip:** When hyper-jumping from system to system, the FSD should not be activated while the fuel scoop is deployed and active because this could cause too much heat while charging the FSD, resulting in module damage. Make sure your fuel scoop is retracted and you are some distance away from a major heat source like a main star.

6.2.1.5 Life support

The life support module is selectable exclusively in terms of quality, the size is given on a ship type basis.

The quality differs only in regard to the time you receive an emergency oxygen supply in case either your regular life support system fails (by lack of energy or module damage) or in case your canopy cracks open due to mechanical or kinetic weapon damage.

In the "civilized" parts of the galaxy it is not necessary to provide more life support than "D". If the regular life support or the cockpit glazing fail, there is more than enough time to fly to the next station. As an explorer in remote systems, however, even an "A" module is not sufficient to enable a safe return, so "D" as the lightest option in terms of weight and mostly the best choice.

Only if energy is extremely scarce, an 'E' is sometimes appropriate for life support. Just keep in mind that 'E' life support modules are a bit tight in terms of time available to find a save haven.

One special case should also be mentioned: supposedly contradictory, but conclusive on careful consideration: When the (regular) life support is switched off, no more electricity is needed for it. If one does not assume that the cockpit glazing will fail, but rather that the life supply will be deliberately switched off, then the power is no longer needed. This reduces the heat emitted by the power plant and thus prolongs the "cold" phase when using silent running. The bonus is only marginal, but there are commanders who seriously turn off life support in silent running ships before doing combat. Apart from the ship creating less heat, the 'immersion' when breathing oxygen in a space helmet is somehow adding to the experience – so does the oxygen timer to depletion...

6.2.1.6. Sensors

Sensors are only selectable in quality, their size is given ona per ship basis. The quality of the sensors is mainly about their range.

For 'regular' usage in PvE (Player vs. Environment) (and quite often also in PvP (Player vs. Player)), quality 'D' with the lowest weight and only slightly more power consumption than the standard quality 'E' is usually preferable.

Each level above "D" adds an enormous amount of power consumption and weight, so that larger sensors should only be used if the Horizons package is available and you can reduce the weight of the module with the help of the engineers.

6.2.1.7. Fuel Tank

The fuel tank on most ships can only be adjusted slightly, usually one or two size classes smaller than standard are avilable, with each step reducing fuel capacity by 50%.

Reducing the fuel tank's capacity only makes sense for all-purpose ships that are equipped as combat ships (and rarely for smaller trade vessels to increase jump range). All-purpose ships usually have more range than you need in the (mostly local) combat area.

Under no circumstances should you reduce the tank size of combat ships, these are usually already very tightly calculated and just enough to reach combat, fight and return safely.

6.2.2 Optional Modules

You're completely free in selecting and installing modules which go into the 'optional' module section. Of course, it is rarely advisable to leave all available module slots free. In addition certain module combinations make no real sense, but the freedom to build a ship without a shield generator or a ship with large fuel tanks, for example, can be really useful.

In general, the larger slots for the more important modules are used for the more urgently needed modules. In the case of a freighter, for example, for freight racks, in the case of a battleship for shields. But sometimes you also deviate from this rule, for example if a smaller shield has enough power for the expected opponent – which is quite often the case on ships like the Federal Corvette, the Imperial Cutter or the Fer-de-Lance, but you want to keep more shield capacity in reserve: Then an extra large shield cell bank may supplement the somewhat smaller shield generator.

Important with the optional modules is, among other things, to make sure that you do not "bunker" weight without having to do so. Quickly you have built in 2 or 3 large hull reinforcements or an additional tank you don't really need, which spoil the fun by reducing agility or reduce the jump distance unnecessarily, which makes going places a real pain.

6.2.2.1 AFW - Automatic Field Maintenance Unit

The field maintenance unit is a tool that is unfortunately found far too often in combat ships and rarely in ships that need it: Explorers. Although it also offers the possibility to repair individual modules without docking at a station, this is not possible with combat ships in combat and after a fight you are usually not too far from a station providing instant repairs.

For combat ships, the AFW only makes sense if the commander is an 'endurance fighter': Anyone who spends hours with ships without ammunition (lasers only or plasma accelerators/rail guns modified to consume ship fuel for generating ammunition) and without the need for new shield cells (using fast recharge bi-weave shield) in combat zones or resource zones may enjoy a small AFW.

In general, however, if you suffer module damage in combat against NPC, you should change the conditions to your favor, because module damage in combat is 'one step from the abyss' (especially if it was inflicted on yourself by overheating)!

For explorers, the situation is different: Here the AFM unit is an indispensable component of the equipment on longer distances, since regular wear down and additional stress on modules slowly makes them go belly up if not repaired from time to time.

(We're talking about distances over 20.000 ly here, not the short trip to the space grocery with these yummy Avocados near Trappist-1...)

The module qualities and sizes differ above all in the number of 'ammunition'. For some magical reason, the AFM unit has no weight of its own.

Three things of importance when using the AFM

1.) The AFM cannot repair power plants, so these should always be selected in "A" design for best integrity. In theory, "B" power plants still have a few percent more integrity, but they add up so much weight supplement that most explorers are gratefully against it.

2.) The AFM can't repair hull damage. For this purpose you can carry repair limpets, which if sent out without a target, will repair your own ship. Modules cannot be repaired with repair limpets, but a damaged (not: destroyed) cockpit can be.

3.) The AFM should not be used on the thrusters while in supercruise. Oh, that was clear, because the AFM unit shuts the module down for repairs? Say you would have thought about that...

> **Tip:**
> If the AFM drops back to 0% integrity and can no longer be used: Reboot/repair ship in the right cockpit view. After 1-3 attempts the module gets more than 0% integrity and can be used again to repair other modules. Want to make sure you got a repair option no matter what? Install two small AFMs instead of a single large one. These can repair each other if necessary.

The AFM unit does not need to be assigned to a fire button to use. Simply open the module screen on the right side of the ship (default: key "4") and select the repair option for the respective module. Do not forget to check: The module must be set to "ON" after repair, otherwise there will be nasty surprises.

6.2.2.2. Collector Limpet Controller

Collector limpet controllers, together with their corresponding 'ammunition' – limpets – are used to collect floating objects from space.

They're often used in mining scenarios when they reliably and for quite some time collect every mining object in your ship's vicinity.

For 'bring in everything you can see' mode just do not target any object. By targetting something, a limpet will be programmed to bring in this object, then die. Not targetting lets them live longer and bring in multiple objects.

Collector limpet controller qualities (letters: 'A' - 'E') primarily describe the limpets' service life, but can also (especially in quality 'B') differ in range. 'A' quality, for example, has the best overall characteristics in terms of service life, 'B', however, has a slightly higher range.

When deploying all types of limpets, note that their speed is limited. Your own ship's speed should be under 200m/s to prevent a collision.

If your limpets don't collect anything, check that your cargo scoop is deployed – this opens your cargo hatch for receiving incoming limpets which just idle in some kind of delivery queue if the cargo hatch is closed (cargo scoop retracted).

6.2.2.3 Prospector Limpet Controller

Prospector limpet controllers, together with their corresponding 'ammunition' – limpets – are used to check asteroids for valuable ore.

If you fire a reconnaissance limpet at an asteroid with the help of the control unit previously assigned to a fire button, the limpet will fly to the point you are currently aiming for – which should be an asteroid.

Once deployed, you can manually target the limpet (Standard-key: 'T' for target-ahead) and watch it impact the astreroid.
Once the limpet has arrived, you can see the asteroid's contents on the small left info pane in forward view: all minable ores in percentages and additional information in case the asteroid has fissures and can be blown up using seismic charges because of existing deposits of deep core materials.

Prospector limpet controllers are available in size class 1 (one active limpet each), size class 3 (two active limpets each), size class 5 (four active limpets each) and size class 7 (eight active limpets each). Any size bigger than class 1 only makes sense if you are trained in handling multiple limpets at a time, since only one can be manually switched on as a target.

One word out of experience: Using a prospector limpet controller above size 3 is a waste. No exception.

The qualities (letters from A - E) describe not only the range but also the service life of the drones. You normally use "A" modules, but "B" modules can also be useful in individual cases: Just compare the data and select according to your area of application.
Find 'ammunition' for this controller by selecting "Extended Maintenance" and then "Filling". Paste to all controllers.

When deploying all types of limpets, note that their speed is limited. Your ship should go 200m/s or slower to prevent a collision which could render the limpet inoperable.

6.2.2.4 Decontamination Limpet Controller

Decontamination limpets are gold when hunting Thargoids. If you're not into doing so, you won't need them.

With decontamination limpets, the outer skin of a ship is freed from alien artifacts (slime!) that damage the hull.

The Thargoid hunt is too extensive to be dealt with in the beginner's book. Soon there will be more in a seperate part.

6.2.2.5 Frame Shift Drive (FSD) Interdictor

To engage other ships – no matter if human or NPC – one needs to meet them in normal speed mode.

For pulling a ship out of supercruise into normal speed mode, there is a broad variety of FSD interdictor modules available.

Like other modules, the FSD interdictor module is also available in different sizes and qualities. They primarily differ in range: the better the quality (letter) and the bigger the size (number) the more distance (in seconds to reach the target, not in light seconds) an FSD interdictor can handle.

Apart from the given range, size and quality of the module determines its integrity (longevity) which is usually of less interest as you won't tend to interdict other ships with your own ship being damaged previously.

Frame shift drive interdictors do have mass, though. You can either go for a 'D' rated FSD interdictor in one size or for a slightly (usually ca. 30%) heavier version one size smaller. It all depends on your personal choice regarding using a smller or bigger module slot for this device.

In other words: If you're not interdicting lots of targets in a row, go for a small sized interdictor of 'D' quality. Not very comfortable in terms of range, but it does the job.

> **FYI:**
> All tales about bigger FSD interdictors providing a better interdiction result or less damage to the ship or better coffee or better digestion or more hair are urban legends.

When activating the FSD interdictor, it is important that its range is not defined as a fixed distance, but in terms of time for reaching target. In practice this means: If you are faster than your 'victim', this gives you an advantage even if you hunt at a greater distance. So if you're planning to pull ships out of supercruise speed mode, first create a bit of a distance to your opponent, then close in fast. If you pursue an opponent going away from the gravitational pull of a planet, you will probably die of old age before your interdictor indicates that your opponent is in range, even if he is directly in front of you. Because of his starting position further away from the planet – less gravity, more speed - he is always a little faster than you are.

The better you adjust your speed, the more agility you got in supercruise speed mode. Ideally, you use approx. 40% of the maximum attainable speed, represented by the bars on the throttle. Place the thrust at about 40% of the maximum speed if you need to maneuver to get into interdiction position behind your "victim".

6.2.2.6. Cargo Racks

These have no mass and they consume no energy. If you have empty module bays it is never a mistake to install cargo racks.

> **Tip:**
> Especially with the lower ranks and outside of missions you can relatively safely skip on using shields, especially if you have carefully read the most important tips in 'survival' section of this book. This significantly increases the maximum cargo capacity and thus the profit per flight, especially for smaller ships.

6.2.2.7. Hatch Breaker Limpet Controller

If you wish to 'borrow' other ships' cargo, you need to open their cargo hatch in flight as most of NPC and human players stick to their belongings and see no use in providing you with free cargo.

The more raw way of opening a cargo hatch is opening fire at a ship until its shields have dropped, then aiming at the cargo hatch module until its integrity is low enough to fail. It then drops all cargo from the cargo hold.

The main problem with this approach is, that some ships will explode by 'collateral' damage done while trying to damage the cargo hatch.

The more professional and more effective way is using a hatch breaker limpet controller. At low to medium ship speeds (up to about 200 m/s) you can send limpets on a hunt for other people's cargo hatch (beware! This is considered a hostile act!).

Simply target the enemy (no need to target a submodule like the cargo hatch, just target the ship), then try to fly as slow as possible but at least below 500 m/s (hatch breaking limpets are faster than usual limpets) when 'firing' a hatch breaker limpet towards your enemy. Make sure having a fire button assigned to the hatch breaker limpet controller before engaging ships!

6.2.2.8. Flight Assists

Automation has found its place in space travel.

There are three class 1 sized modules available to make your daily life easier - or at least less complex.

1E Standard Docking Computer

The 'minimalist' version of the flight assist modules. When near a station with an active landing clearance, just throttle down to 0% thrust (Standard key: 'X'). The standard docking computer module will then attempt to dock you on the assigned pad without killing you.

1E Advanced Docking Computer

In addition to the standard version's capability of docking you more or less safe at stations and settlements, this advanced module provides (more or less) safe undocking manouevres.

As with using the docking function, for undocking just provide a 0% thrust setting and enjoy the show.

1E Supercruise Assist

This module is not a replacement for the docking computers above, it's an additional module for autopiloting functions in supercruise speed mode.

Supercruise Assist is activated by either targetting a planet – which will result in your ship orbitting this planet after approaching it – or by targetting a station or another 'target' – which will result in your ship approaching that target until dropping to normal speed mode.

> **CAUTION!** If you are using Horizons and attempt to approach a ground settlement using the Supercruise Assist module, make sure you approach the settlement from the right side (regular not dotted circle). If the settlement is on the other side of the planet the Supercruise Assist module will approach it in a direct path...)

Activation of Supercruise Assist differs from the docking und undocking procedures. You need to place your throttle 'in the blue' for activation after using the Assist option in your NAV menu on the left side, then align your ship toward your target. Instead of simply locking a target, you choose the second option from the left to activate Supercruise Assist mode)

> **CAUTION!** After dropping at your target, your throttle setting persists. You will move ahead with medium speed, which is basically a dangerous thing as you might collide with other ships or stations. Take care!

And a word about skill: If you don't plan to repeatedly fly loop trade routes or similar, skip installing these modules.

Not only do you need the skills of fast and secure docking and undocking, you can also bring the used class 1 slots to better use. The small slots do not look like much, but by placing less important stuff like interdictors in it, you often make room for bigger module slots which then can be used for cargo or defense. Think about it!

> **FYI**
> Flight assist modules are THE ONE identifier for "easy prey" in pirate and ganker circles (and among those whose greatest fun it is to rob others of their well deserved ships). So, especially when in the "open" game mode: Leave your flight assists at home.

6.2.2.10. Module Reinforcements

Modules all have a defined "integrity", i.e. the ability to "collect" a certain amount of damage before they temporarily or even permanently give up function.

If you lose your shield protection in combat, if the shield generator is too small (always check mass values when installing one) or if you even started without a shield generator, enemy hits will damage the ship modules at the place where you are hit. But not only that, proficient fighters even specifically attack modules such as the power plant or the thrusters to paralyze them.

This cannot be prevented with module reinforcements forever, but the survival time of these - usually very important - modules can be significantly increased.

Module reinforcements are available in sizes (numbers) from class 1 up to class 5. Each class generally offers about 50% more protection, but comes with a 100% weight increase for each size bigger. It is therefore advisable (especially for smaller ships) to pay very close attention to how much protection you really need. Class 5 weighs 16 tons.

The module reinforcements are available in two qualities, 'D' and 'E'. Quality 'D' absorbs 60% of the module damage caused upon your ship until the module reinforcement is exhausted. Then 100% of the incoming module damage reaches the module.

Quality 'E' is not recommended. Although it is cheaper, its low quality absorbs only 30% of the module damage caused to the ship.

First rule of outfitting applies: Keep your ship's weight down. In general, modules that have not been modified by engineers rarely have above '100' in integrity.

This means that the module is definitely to be considered defective when it has taken "100" of the damage.

If a module gain of quality "D" is used, 40% of the module damage is generated on the module, 60% is absorbed by the module protection module. In other words, with '100' integrity on the module with ample module reinforcement, your enemy needs about '250' damage to destroy the module: 60% (150 damage) is absorbed by the reinforcement, and 40% (100 damage) bleeds through to your module(s) which should be protected. After that, your module is 'dead'.

Conversely, this also means that a module protection of over '250' makes no sense if you only have modules that can suffer a maximum of '100' in damage, because you would have lots of module protection left over but inside, your targetted module would be toast.

For this reason, the general rule for real combat ships: module integrity x 1.5 = module protection size. Mostly about "150", a single "3D" module reinforcement package is sufficient.

> **Tip:**
> If you have the option, use two module reinforcements with a total value of "150", one of which is significantly smaller than the other. This offers the same overall protection with less weight, but more importantly, if the smaller module gain fails, you will be warned by the ship! This 'wake up call' can be used as a last hint as in "Get out of here, or this will end badly!"

6.2.2.11. Detailed Surface Scanner

Against all logic, this small (size class 1) module is not to be found in the utility area but in the optional module area.

The detailed surface scanner is used for closer examination of planetary objects and rings. On the one hand to map surfaces of planets (lucrative, a detailed surface scan of an earth-like planet can earn 600,000 credits for a single object - and more!). On the other hand, it is used to discover lucrative "hot spots" on planetary rings: deposits of very expensive, degradable goods.

Using the detailed surface scanner seems to be very difficult at first, but once accustomed it turns out to be surprisingly simple to use: after having flown close to a planet (about 0.1 ls away), one first switches to the FSS cockpit mode (default: blue color). Then one activates the surface scanner. (Keys for this are usually not preset, please use the key assignments in the main menu options.)

When the surface scanner view is activated, you first see the planet in front of you. You are close enough when the indicated distance to the target planet has just changed from light seconds (ls) to millions of meters (Mm). Depending on the size of the planet, the planet is almost filling your frontal view. Now you can fire probes at the planet (or its ring).
In order to map the planet completely, one either "shoots" probes "area-wide" at a distance dependent on the position and size of the planet and at different appropriate angles onto it - or one changes the position after covering the front hemisphere and moves - time-consuming - to the other side.

To scan the ring for mining valuable materials, you only need a single probe that hits the ring. The hot spots then quickly become visible.

> **Tip:**
> To map the planet in one go to 100% (necessary for the name tag in the card and the maximum payout), first cover the visible "front" half of the planet with probes.

Then you have to try to reach the back of the planet with the probes without changing your position. You use gravity to do that. If you aim further out the probes first fly slightly away from the planet and are then attracted to it over time.

For planets with rings, the note "Ring" is also very helpful when aiming. You simply aim as close as possible to the ring without hitting it, i.e. on the side of the ring facing the planet you just miss the ring. This technique almost always works without much practice!

Then you have to try to reach the back of the planet with the probes without changing your position. You use gravity to do that. If you aim further out the probes first fly slightly away from the planet and are then attracted to it over time. For planets with rings, the note "Ring" is also very helpful when aiming. You simply aim as close as possible to the ring without hitting it, i.e. on the side of the ring facing the planet you just miss the ring. This technique almost always works without much practice!

6.2.2.12. Passenger Cabins

Passenger cabins are needed for the - lucrative - transport of passengers. These can be purchased in grades of Economy, Business, First and Luxury classes. Luxury cabins can only be installed in passenger ships and for these you need at the Horizons DLC Pass. (No worries, luxury cabins are rarely useful. Read on.)

Depending on trade rank, combat rank and explorer rank, and your reputation with the small mission-giving faction(s) at the station you are located, you will be offered different kinds of missions. In addition, the mission offer also differs in the question of how prosperous the system is in which you are just looking for passengers and of course in what state the local economy there currently is.

A lot of factors, but only one really important advice: Before equipping your ship with passenger cabins, take a close look what kind of missions (Cabin class, number of passengers, distance to go) your mission givers usually offer. Read the mission offers in detail and be precise. Only then do you decide how many cabins and what quality of service you offer. The 'will do and try' approach is a guarantee for a minimal income and lots of frustrations.

> **Tip:** Passengers can be all kind of people. Careful when transporting criminals. They are a magnet for assassination attempts and being scanned with them on board can become a costly endeavour. Avoid scans, drop heatsinks when needed... or skip these missions.

6.2.2.13. Planetary Vehicle Hangars

Currently there are four versions of "SRV" hangars for the Horizons DLC package, which includes planetary landings on non-atmospheric planets. Class (size) 2 and 4. Qualities 'G' and 'H'.

Class 2 hangars include one SRV, class 4 hangars include two SRV.

Quality 'G' is much lighter, but requires much more power than quality 'H'. However, this can almost always be neglected because the hangar module can conveniently be set to priority "5" in the right in ship window's module settings table. The hangar is therefore of secondary importance in terms of power supply and is simply switched off in the event of increased power requirements (e.g. when your weapons are deployed).

After all, landing and exploring is not necessarily done with the weapons extended.

The important thing is that the hangar is just ... a hangar. Please remember to buy an SRV vehicle after buying the hangar! Nothing is more frustrating than finding out at your destination that you have bought a hangar but there's no vehicle to use.

6.2.2.14. Refineries

A refinery is needed to convert fragments of valuable ore from mining areas and hot spots into sellable cargo. Refineries are available in sizes from '1' to '4' and qualities from 'A' to 'E'. They differ only in the number of 'baskets' or 'slots'.

It is important to note that one rule applies to almost all refineries: 'minus one size class plus one quality class".

A '4E' refinery is therefore approximately equivalent to a '3D' refinery or a '2C' refinery. Since the refineries all magically have no weight and only differ in power consumption (the more 'A' the more electricity consumption), the larger size (number) should be given priority over the supposedly better quality. If you have enough room. Consolation: The difference in electricity consumption is not really big.

The number of baskets/slots is of varying importance. If one specifically goes hunting for valuable materials in the deep core of individual asteroids ("deep core mining"), a tiny refinery is sufficient, since rarely more than one material is incoming at a time. If the core contains a different material, simply empty the basket(s) by hand in the refinery menu (right in-ship-window, standard key "4") and continue operation.

If you proceed "classically" and splinter fragments of asteroids (e.g. Painit) with a mining laser, a larger refinery is advantageous, because each asteroid has its own composition and in small refineries you spend a huge part of your time cleaning the refinery of unused fragments. This can considerably slow down the mining process and due to its repetitiveness it can burn you out quite fast.

6.2.2.15. Repair Limpet Controller

Repair Limpet Controllers are available in size classes 1, 3, 5 and 7 in all regular quality steps (A - E).

For each size class you get the possibility to use one more limpet at the same time, i.e. with class 1 a single one, with class 7 up to four.

The qualities offer different ranges.

For most applications a class 1 control unit is sufficient. Control units are quite heavy and thus associated with limitations in range and agility of the ship. So this is a great place to save some money (and weight). The number of limpets carried is much more important than the number of controllers or the maximum number of limpets to use at a time. All that because a limpet is used and occupied for each repair operation so limpet count is the limiting factor.
The drones are activated like other drones: You assign a fire button to the control unit and simply 'fire' it. Once a target is connected, it is repaired. If you don't have a target locked, the limpet will diligently 'attack' your ship and repair all damage found.

6.2.2.16. Hull Reinforcement Packages

The ship's hull is often the "last resort" when shields fail in battle.

Instead of using heavy and expensive bulkheads (see above), it is a good idea (always assuming you have enough optional module space) to use hull reinforcement packages (modules).

These are available in sizes 1-5 and in qualities 'D' and 'E'.

Clear recommendation: Never use 'E'. Although nearly as strong as 'D' reinforcements and much cheaper, they're twice as heavy. Range and agility of your ship will suffer considerably!

Since, analogous to the module reinforcements, each size class bigger only brings a slight increase in protection which is in turn disproportionately bringing with it an increase in module mass. The best "power-to-weight ratio" is either '1D' (for a minimum weight) or '3D' for maximum protection with still bearable weight. In other words: Use '1D' reinforcements if you just wish to enhance your hull a bit and '3D' reinforcements if you consider hull strength a vital factor on your ship without being willing to sacrifice agility and range.

'4D' and '5D' should only be used on large ships and if you really want that much hull protection. Please keep in mind: Especially in a fight against a human commander the modules have often failed for a long time when there's lots of hull left. You need to act wisely with shields down for not exposing vital 'organs' of your ship to enemy fire.

6.2.2.17. Collector Limpet Controllers

Instead of collecting cargo and other materials by hand - which is hard work and can be bothersome at times - you can use collection limpet controllers.

These controllers use regular limpets – buy them in 'advanced maintenance – restock' please – for collecting objects from space. Target something, fire a limpet, enjoy the show. It will bring in the object, then die. Do not target anything when firing a collector limpet and enjoy your little minion bringing in everything in range until time-of-life of the little critter expires.

The control unit required for this is available in size classes '1'-'7' and qualities 'A'-'E'. The size classes differ above all in the number of simultaneously active drones, the qualities above all in service life and range.

As with the other limpet controllers, a closer look at different types can be helpful: 'B' type limpet controllers usually provide more range on limpets than 'A' controllers and the cheap 'E' controllers can sometimes be a better choice than 'D' controllers.

In order to collect objects please assign a fire button to the controller. The limpets bought before undocking ('advanced maintenance – restock).

6.2.2.18. Shield Generators

Shield generators are, so to speak, the "foremost front" against external influences.

If the installed shield generator is sufficiently dimensioned (minimum mass of the generator exceeds the actual total mass of the ship) the ship is completely shielded against module damage from the outside and the hull is also safe from external influences.

With a small limitation: So-called "phasing-effect modified" lasers and plasma accelerators, which cause damage to the hull when your shields are still intact. However, they will only be used by NPC in the upper echelons, missions and conflict zones and should not be regarded as the rule even by human players. The modification to a phase-modified laser or plasma accelerator considerably reduces the damage of these weapons, which makes only a small fraction of players even consider using this effect. Nonetheless, check your hull after the first few shots on you. If its integrity is reduced you can be sure you're being attacked with phasing weapons.

If the shield generator is too small, the hull and modules are "passed through" a portion of the damage that hits the shields. As a result, you may be out of action or destroyed long before the shields fail.

Therefore please always pay attention to use a shield generator of a sufficient size in regard to your ship's mass and if there is no room for a sufficient generator, simply consider the use of a module protection package to at least compensate a bit for bleed through damage.
Running shields which don't cover 100% of your ship's mass can be a viable option if you don't encounter too many or too strong enemies and need your bigger module slots for things that are more important to you and your current mission, cargo racks for example.

For purely civilian operation without expected stronger opponents (no combat, no missions), a 'D' shield of the largest installable class (or the class that covers the entire expected ship mass) is sufficient in most cases. A 'D' shield offers significantly less protection than an 'A' shield, but saves a lot of weight which in turn provides more range and more agility – and saves you a lot of money. If you're more or less trained in 'dodging' incoming attacks, go for 'D' shields if not planning heavy combat. Don't use them in fights, though.

'A' shields are the basis for most combat ships (see exceptions at the end of this section). They offer the most protection at high costs and high power consumption, which can then be extended with shield boosters (utility modules) and other tricks (engineers, guardians - both in the Horizons package).

In general, when selecting the right shield generator, you should have a feeling for how much damage your opponents will inflict on you. Ideally, you should choose your shield generator so that an attack wave (the time in which you fire your weapons until your 'WEP' energy/heat bucket is empty and the time in which you cause maximum damage to your opponent) consumes a maximum of 50% of your shields.

Your damage on shields is then recharged ('healed') with a shield cell, which contains quite exactly this expected damage. So you have a (nearly) maximum filled shield at your disposal the next time you start an attack wave. Your shields are always filled when attacking and under fire and you're 100% safe until you finally wrecked your opponent.

For larger ships, the 50% consideration is omitted, as the shields of larger ships (especially those improved by engineers) can withstand far more than an attack wave of average enemies. For example, your starter ship, the (in-)famous Sidewinder comes with about 50 MJ shield protection, an average equipped allround cargo cutter with some engineering work provides at least 1000 MJ 'raw' shield protection. (Some combat ships have 7000 MJ and more 'raw' shield protection with the help of the engineers). At this point, the note is also displayed:

PvP, i.e. a fight 'commander' against 'commander' should not take place if one of the two participants is not at the same 'tuning' level in terms of utilizing the enormous advantages provided by Horizons' 'engineers'. You will rarely win a fight against an engineered ship without using engineering for yours.

Shields not improved by engineers have an imbalance in protection against various types of damage. A shield with 100 MJ 'raw' damage (damage caused by ramming and collisions of any kind (or by weapons with a high damage rate of this kind such as rail guns or plasma accelerators) has only about 80 MJ 'resistance' to thermal weapons such as lasers.
Wish to damage other people unengineered shields? Use lasers.

In regard to damage done by kinetic weapons (cannons and guns of all kinds) there is a higher resistance, shields offer almost 60% more protection, in our example almost 160 MJ. Being attacked by an enemy using kinetic weapons your shields will withstand a lot more damage.

Compared to explosive weapons (torpedoes, rockets), shields are really very capable even in an unimproved condition: Our exemplary '100 MJ' shield offers almost 90% more defense in regard to explosive attacks - that's about 190 MJ!

So whoever has the 'shields up' has to worry less about cannons of all kinds and less about explosive attacks. By the way, this usually looks the other way around with 'shields down'.

Besides the regular shield generators there are two special shields:

<u>1.) Bi-Weave Shield Generators</u>

These shield generators are classified as quality 'C', which is close to it but somehow completely wrong, too: Their performance always corresponds exactly to the performance of the 'D' quality of the same size, with the weight of 'A'. What makes these shields so special is their ability to replenish themselves faster (up to twice as fast as an 'A' shield) and return to basic operation faster once they've fallen (up to 50% faster than an 'A' shield).

Bi-Weave shields are the means of choice for ships that are able to continue fighting well in the event of a fallen shield because they are agile enough to be positioned in a way in which the enemy is not able to hit vital modules, because of having enough hull reserves and because of being well protected in terms of module damage in general.

A Cobra Mk3, for example, can go bounty hunting using a Bi-Weave shield and plenty of hull reinforcements. This with a lot of endurance as long as the 'commander' is a little cautious. He simply avoids heavy module damage when shields drop, uses a bit of his ship's well built hull and module protection (added hull and module reinforcement packages) and heals his shields in no time once the current enemy is defeated.

This is a useful tactic as the Cobra's standard shields provide little more than 75MJ of protection, which is less than 10% of a 'hull & bi weave' built Cobra Mk 3.

So Bi-Weave are very popular shields for "endurance" bounty hunters. In addition, they are often used on so-called "hybrid" ships, some of which fight at crawl speed, or on so-called "hull monsters", where the shield is simply used as a constantly regenerating additional protection.

2) "Prismatic Shields"

These shield generators are only available after you have "served" a few weeks with one of the PowerPlay characters, in this case: Aisling Duval.

Prismatic shields are well worth the effort. Although they're heavy and draw a lot of energy, they're not only good 'heavy duty' shields in general, they're the basis for a lot of 'shield tank' builds when doing PvP or combat in general.
Their high cost and the short 'window of opportunity' in purchasing them (you need to still be pledged to Aisling Duval when buying them, imagine buying a class 8 shield generator for your 'Future Cutter' on stock while still using some small sized ship...) makes me emphasize: Do not pledge for these shields unless you got the money for a broad collection of 'on stock' shield generators of all sizes.

Another drawback of prismatic shield generators is their abysmally bad regeneration rate. Shield generators need more time to 'come back to life' the bigger they are and they need more and more time to refill to 100% the bigger they are. Prismatics add insult to injury by reducing rebuild rate and regeneration rate even further. With a big prismatic shield generator you are in for waiting 30 minutes or more until back at 100% of strength. This makes them almost unfeasable for usage in resource zones and other situations with multiple targets in a row.

Access to individual engineers available in the Horizons Pack can greatly enhance the performance of shield generators. Among other things, this is due to the fact that on ships with many utility slots, the shield boosters, which may be installed in large numbers, can increase the resistance against damage enormously. Thus, for example shield strengths of 14000 (!) MJ against lasers - and even more - are not a rare sight.

6.2.2.19. Shield Cell Banks

With 'empty' shields after or in the midst of a fight, one would like to see some magic at hand for refilling these in an instant.

This magic is called a shield cell bank.

Shield cells can not reactivate 'dropped' shields, but when used in time they can recharge a huge portion or the whole shield capacity in a few seconds.
Shield cell banks are available in all conceivable module sizes and qualities (1 - 8 and A - E).

The choice of the right shield cell bank is not easy. You have to take into account how much capacity your shields have, how much energy and weight you can invest on installed shield cell banks, how to handle their heat and in which situations you plan to use them.

For smaller ships, the rule of thumb is "one class smaller than the shield used". If you follow this, you should ideally also install a heat sink launcher in the tool slots, which is activated manually at the same time or ideally even 2-3 seconds before firing a shield cell bank.

If you like to handle things with more precision, take a look at the "raw" shield value (shield health) in the right in-ship info window - (standard key "4") and then decide how big your shield cell should be. In Coriolis, you can easily display the total capacity of the shield cells used and then select a size that, for example, fills 1/3 of the capacity. Then you trigger a shield cell bank every time you lose one of the three shield rings.

As a rule one prefers a 'better' quality (i.e. rather A instead of B instead of C etc.) instead of a larger class (i.e. rather class 1A instead of 2D instead of 3E etc). Reason for this is the fact, that the size (number) of the shield cell bank determines the amount of heat generated on activation. The bigger the class, the more heat it generates. On a Cobra Mk 3, for example, a Class 2 shield cell can be used without additional cooling of your ship by using installed heatsinks, as long as you neither boost or fire weapons 2-3 seconds before igniting the shield cell bank and during the shield cell bank's active recharge phase.
Depending on size and class, shield cells have a different number of triggerable individual cells (as in 'ammo capacity').

'D' shield cells have the lowest weight, however with a cruel decrease in recharge capability and 'B' shield cells do hav ethe biggest overall capacity of their class/size because of their huge ammo count – unfortunately, 'B' is also coming with a huge weight penalty.

Overall, 'A' rated shield cells fitting to your shield generator's capacity are the wisest choice with few exceptions.

6.2.2.20. Fuel Scoops

Mankind's greatest dream comes true: Free fuel.

As already described in the beginning of this book, a fuel scoop can refuel at all systems which have a "main sequence" main star of classes KGBFOA and M... free of charge.

For this you simply fly a little closer (not too close) to the main star with the installed fuel scoop automatically deploying... and soon you'll see infos about the amount of fuel scooped per time and your current heat in percent.
Too far away and refueling will be very slow or your fuel scoop could even retract. Too close and it gets too hot fast. One should not go higher than 80% heat while refuelling as especially when getting closer, heat can rise further up. Never leave your ship unattended when refuelling and always check your heat. The moment it rises above 80%, create some distance between that main star and yourself – for your own safety!

Fuel collectors are classified in a simplified way: More size is more performance and 'A' is better than 'B' is better than 'C'... the choice between fuel scoops of similar performance in different sizes and qualities depends on the size of optional module slot you can use for the fuel scoop and the amount of money you are willing to pay.

On a Cobra Mk3 for example, the biggest fuel scoop you can install is a class 4A. It has about 342 kg per second fuel flow and its cost is about 2.9 million credits. While 'going places' in a rush, you need about 10 seconds on average to reposition your ship while in close vicinity of a main star. You will therefore scoop at least 3420kg = 3.4 tons of fuel each time you 'meet' a KGBFOAM star.

The maximum fuel needed for a single jump (and rarely used 100%) for a 4A frame shift drive on a Cobra Mk3 is 3 tons.
Using the 4A fuel scoop you will therefore fill up your tanks completely by using KGBFOAM stars. Even if travelling around places which contain scoopable stars every 1-3 hops, you are absolutely safe and comfortable in travelling using a 4A fuel scoop.

For regular use and 'not running dry' (keep in mind: https://fuelrats.com) you only need a small fuel scoop. In theory, a ca. 300 credits scoop in class 1E is enough (although it only scoops about 18 kg/s, which translates in nearly 15 minutes to refill a dry tank). Using a 1A scoop in the same small module slot costs about 82.000 credits, but with a flow of about 42 kg/s you're filled up to 100% in about 6.5 minutes.

If you would like to have the same flow rate as a 1A fuel scoop (42 kg/s), but you can 'waste' a class 2 module slot for this task, you could opt for a 2D fuel scoop (43 kg/s) that comes with a much lower cost: About 4.500 credits instead of 82.000 credits with the 1A.

If money is no problem, you can just max out that optional module slot, using a 2A fuel scoop with 75 kg/s and a cost of ca. 285.000 credits.

Lots of options. Just weigh them and consider money needed (and rebuy in case you get destroyed, keep in mind an 8A fuel scoop (Imperial Cutter sized) costs around 289 million credits which results in about 15 million additional rebuy cost in case that ship gets destroyed) and what kind of module slot you can use.

> **Tip:**
> Use coriolis.io for these decisions – with real life numbers everything becomes much clearer than after reading some page in here.

6.2.2.21. Fuel tanks

Fuel tanks are not a substitute for fuel scoops.

Seriously. This sentence is quite important because you can way too often see ships that have installed huge fuel tanks with a lot of weight for longer distances instead of using the weightless fuel collectors. This reduces jump range and increases number of jumps needed to destination. Not wise.

Most non-battleships have a large enough fuel reservoir to refuel all 3-4 jumps at the appearing star of the KGBFOA or M category.

Simply check your fuel consumption per jump (coriolis.io). For journeys within the inhabited area, ships which have enough fuel for 4 jumps in a row without running dry are completely hassle-free (as long as you carry a small fuel scoop with you!)

If you travel to the less populated parts of the galaxy (outside the inhabited bubble) you will occasionally enter areas where these main sequence stars - KGBFOAM - become rare. In that case you will be quite glad for some extra fuel carried with you.

Many explorers therefore install fuel tanks with a size needed for about 8-10 jumps in order to play it safe. Thus after half of the maximum jumps possible (check: fuel gauge at approx. 50%) the tank is filled up. If no star is found to refuel, open the galactic map and make sure that one of the next jumps is a main sequence star before you run dry.

Notice:
- Largest fuel scoop possible
- Fuel tank 4+ jumps for regular usage
- Fuel tank 8+ jumps for exploration

6.2.2.22. Fuel Transfer Limpet Controller

This limpet controller is used to supply other ships with additional fuel if necessary.

To refuel another ship, simply install one of these controller and stock several (each one is 1 ton of fuel) limpets in station services menu – advanced maintenance – restock.

Assign the controller to an unused fire button (which doesn't fire at the one you wish to refuel, you get the point...).

Get close (into limpet range), target your 'victim', fire a limpet. Watch it refuel the other ship. Done.

Keep in mind that each ton you send to the other ship is taken out of your fuel tank.

6.2.3 Utility modules

Number count on utility module slots is different on each ship type. The one thing that all ships have in common is the utility slot size being '0' without exception and a simplified quality range from 'A' as in 'best' to 'E' as in 'weakest'.

> **Notice:**
> A = Best performance, highest consumption
> E = Worst performance

6.2.3.1. Chaff Launcher

Available in only one size and version, this module can reduce the accuracy of gimballed and turreted weapons for a few seconds.

After a few seconds, however, the protective effect stops and your opponent gets back all of his weapons' tracking capabilities.

The chaff launcher is best used against opponents without (!) fixed weapons or missiles. In regular combat, chaff is used when the enemy can reach you with his weapons, but keep in mind: Chaff only irritates guided weapons, if you are close by you will still suffer from a huge part of the incoming enemy fire, the bigger your ship (huge target) the worse.

> **Notice:**
> The larger your ship and the smaller the distance to your opponent, the less effective chaff-throwers are.

On most ships (especially those with a small number of utility slots available) there are more important modules than this. After all most enemies (especially NPC or aggressive PvP style commanders) use fixed weapons anyway, especially when ranked high in combat.

If you have lots of utility module slots and you experience attacks from enemies with gimballed or turreted weapons again and again, you can install two chaff dispensers. With an active time of about 10 seconds and a reload time of about 20 seconds, two of these cover the whole fight.

> **Remark**: At festive days, birthdays of commanders or when celebrating larger victories in game, there can be groups of 1-30 commanders near stations simultaneously deploying chaff dispensers. This 'glitter rain' is quite a sight. Try it once!

6.2.3.2 Electronic Counter Measures ECM

The ECM module is intended for temporary defence against (guided) missiles and torpedoes. After assigning the ECM to a fire button and activating it, the ECM starts charging and keeps on doing so as long as its fire button is steadily pressed. Once the fire button is released, the ECM charge is deployed. The longer the button is pressed, the bigger the ECM's range.
Keep in mind an ECM does not kill incoming missiles, it only puts them to sleep for a certain time. After that, the missiles will become 'hot' again. Use that time to get out of range.

A single ECM is not a sufficient defense against missiles due to the long phase of non-usability after being used. You need at least two of these modules if you're expecting massive missile attacks. It is better to generally build ships that can withstand rocket attacks (shields do this to a great extent), and in case of doubt to take the plunge).

6.2.3.3 Experimental Modules

The experimental area is intended for modules used in connection with Thargoids (mostly). This is part of the Horizons package and not covered in scope here. Please wait for the corresponding part of the book series.

6.2.3.4. Pulse Wave Analyser

Essential module for deep core mining.

In contrast to the removal of superficial materials with regular mining lasers and the slow fragmentation of the outermost layer of an asteroid with abrasive lasers, one can go for the rare and very expensive materials in asteroids' cores – therefore the name deep core mining.

The pulse wave analyzer not only shows all promising asteroids for regular mining in the specified range (forward, approx. 60 degrees field of view, maximum range 12 km), it also indicates, more or less reliably, the presence of expensive deep core materials. The latter appear with a very saturated yellow. Closer to the asteroid you can see the fissures where you apply seismic charges to fragmentate the asteroid.

6.2.3.5 Heat Sink

A very helpful, if not almost essential module for most ships and applications is the heatsink.

It is capable of lowering the ship's temperature for a short time by a huge degree. Most ship configurations with an active heat sink reach temperatures below 20% even in combat conditions.

Heat sinks are the lifeline in the event of overheating, which can be dangerous for your modules: This range starts at 100%. At approx. 120%, serious module damage starts, from approx. 200%, even if this amount of heat is only exceeded for a short time, severe module damage or even module failure will occur.

Heat sinks are also used regularly, for example to compensate the heat development of large shield cells. The larger the shield cell and the smaller the ship, the more important it may be to use a heat sink just before using the shield cell(s).

Shortly before using the shield cell because the heat sinks need a short time to lower the heat. After firing the heat sink the heat drops, then the cooling stagnates, then the main part of the cooling follows.

If two separate shield cells are used, the heat sink is therefore activated first. Then in 1-2 seconds distance the first shield cell follows.
Depending on the shield cell, there is now a significant increase in heat, followed by a drop in temperature. When this has found its "bottom", i.e. when the temperature does not drop any further, the second shield cell is fired.

Depending on the shield cells, up to three shield cells with one heat sink can be used when used skilfully.

A special application for heat sinks is 'silent running'. If this is activated, the ship becomes warmer and warmer. If this warming is compensated with a heat sink to lower temperatures below approx. 40%, you become invisible at medium distance for targeted weapons (not for fixed weapons as you will still be visible to the enemy's eye!).

Another application of the heat sinks is smuggling. If you have "unsuitable" goods with you, and you are scanned by the police or a station while smuggling (message on screen!) and you quickly deploy a heat sink without a major delay. This is sufficient to lower the temperature of normal ships to such an extent that the scan remains unsuccessful. You then have a few seconds until the next scan occurs. In the remaining time you can fly into the (bigger) station or land on a pad (outpost). If there's not enough time, just deploy another heat sink.

Just one word of caution: If you need to deploy heatsinks to compensate general heat development or 'hot' weapons, you are doomed. You will run out of these little gems in no time. Change your ship setup!

<u>By the way:</u>
Smuggling is easier the more the station "likes" (reputation!) you and the smaller your ship is.
No matter what ship you're using: Use a maximum of 90% thrust (no boost) and don't 'dance' as in using vector thrusters or radical manoeuvres when near stations. Just fly in gently and the rare scans can be overcome with heat sinks as described above.

6.2.3.6. Point Defense

In contrast to the electronic countermeasures ECM (see 6.2.3.2.), a point defense module is effective without the need for manual activation or intervention.

In principle, it is a small multicannon on a turret that attempts to destroy incoming missiles using ammunition with a high projectile speed.

The point defense is effective against all types of missiles and also all types of limpets.

The weaknesses of the point defense is, on the one hand, that it can only fight objects in sight. If your point defense is mounted on top of the ship and the attack is from below, it can do nothing against approaching objects.

On the other hand the point defense is overwhelmed by swarm missiles (Powerplay weapon 'packhound missile', up to 24 missiles simultaneously on the way to you). These are not to be found on NPC.

NPC missiles are in general only of limited importance against shields. So as long as you don't play against humans, missile defense should only be paid attention to if you plan using a ship without shields or going to ganker infested space. These players usually carry FSD disrupting missiles to block you from escaping their bullying. As these are usually found at engineering bases and community goals only, it's up to you to create some risk assessment.

6.2.3.7. Shield Booster

These very useful utility modules increase the capacity of your shields. They are available in qualities from 'E' to 'A' with 'E' being the weakest in performance but also the lightest in weight and the one with the least power consumption.

Shield boosters increase the shield generators performance by a certain factor. You can imagine them as cups glued to a bucket and connected to it. They increase the total capacity of the bucket, no more and no less. (With engineers' magic in the Horizons package this becomes more complex... and more powerful.)

Please be aware that the efficiency of the individual shield booster types is not the same:

A shield booster 0E delivers 4% more power at 0.2 MJ consumption (20.00% per MJ)
A shield booster 0D delivers 8% more power at 0.5 MJ consumption (16.00% per MJ)
A shield booster 0C delivers 12% more power at 0.7 MJ consumption (17.14% per MJ)
A shield booster 0B delivers 16% more power at 1.0 MJ consumption (16.00% per MJ)
A shield booster 0A delivers 20% more power at 1.2 MJ consumption (16.67% per MJ)

So it is worth taking a look at possible combinations of boosters.

A common and often tragic mistake is the use of shield boosters to achieve more combat endurance. Boosters are not meant to work this way (except when using Engineers later on for special builds of ships). They are intended to increase the basic capacity of a shield to such an extent that one is not constantly in danger of losing one's shields. You shouldn't attempt to increase combat 'stamina' with boosters.

A shield booster of class 0B, for example, delivers a 'bonus' of around 16%, i.e. around 20 MJ, on a Cobra Mk3 with around 125 MJ shield capacity, previously without boosters. This with an additional consumption of 1.0 MJ and a weight of approx. 3 tons.

A Class 2B shield cell bank on the other hand delivers an additional shield capacity of around 210 MJ for the same ship with an additional consumption of around 1.01 MJ and a weight of 4 tons.

A shield cell bank thus delivers significantly more capacity (here: 210 instead of 20 MJ - that is almost 11 times as much!) with the same power consumption and comparable weight. The shield cell bank can of course only deliver this additional defense over a longer period in 'shots' (here: 5), but these are still about 42 MJ in size and thus twice as much as the total capacity of the booster – per shot!

> **Notice:**
> If your shields are big enough for the initial need in defense, but more endurance is desired, then please add shield cells in the optional area instead of wasting valuable power on shield boosters that only help in the first phase of a fight.

6.2.3.8. Frame Shift Wake Scanner

Frame Shift Wake 'clouds' arise when a ship changes speed mode, be it jumping to supercuise mode after undocking from a station or dropping to normal speed mode from supercruise at a station, or be it jumping to another system.

A frame shift wake scanner can be used to analyze 'high wake's (jump to another system).

This is helpful if you want to pursue your target that just ran away from you, either when pirating or on a bounty hunting mission.

A side effect of frame shift wake scanners should be mentioned: The mere fact that you got one installed is proof for certain 'ganker hunters' and 'space cops' to hunt you down. Their line of thought? What for should someone have a frame shift wake scanner installed if not for pursuing the innocent. Take care when near the starter systems or community goals or engineer bases if you got one installed. Expect to be attacked by the less wise.

Most of the time the module slot for the frame shift wake scanner is wasted either way. To find out the target system of a fugitive it is sufficient to do the following: Instead of aiming directly at the fugitive, orient your own ship so that the left hologram of your ship has approximately the same angle to the top right as your own ship in the right hologram has to the top left. As soon as your object of desire has jumped away, you keep exactly this direction and cycle through all accessible systems in your left in ship window's 'navigation' tab (standard key: '1'). Starting from the nearest systems and checking every single system for being present in your forward view. If so, this system most likely is the one your 'prey' jumped to. Go for it.

6.2.3.9. Kill Warrant Scanner

This scanner should actually be called "Destruction Order Scanner", as in the elite universe there is always a functioning rescue capsule available and strictly speaking nobody is killed.

In bounty hunting, the kill warrant scanner adds the bounties a delinquent carries in other systems to the visible local bounty you can cash in on. This increases your income by a huge factor of at least three tiems the original sum. Do not go hunting bounties without a kill warrant scanner ever.

The scanners are available in different sizes (E - A), which differ mostly by range. The smaller scanners are not only cheaper, they also consume only a fraction of the power of the larger models. And this, where the larger models offer only 500m more range per quality level.

For more agile ships in the speed class of over 350 m/s and more a scanner of the class 0D is sufficient, for slower ships a scanner of the class 0C is used. Think about what you can do to your ship for the power saved with a smaller "kill command scanner": better thrusters, better shields, shield cells, and so on:

KW-Scanner 0D: 2.5 km range, 1.3 to, 0.4 MJ, 41.000 cr
KW-Scanner 0A: 4.0 km range, 1.3 to, 3.2 MJ, 1.100.000 mil cr
Difference: 2.8 MJ, 1+ million credits

For comparison: A 6A shield cell bank with 1.840 MJ of additional shield protection is at 2.48 MJ in power consumption. Installing a too large Kill Warrant Scanner is a blatant mistake in equipping ships.

> **Notice:**
> Choose a small "kill command scanner" in order to save power and thus prefer to operate other, more important modules.

6.2.3.10. Manifest Scanner

This module lists the freight list of a scanned ship in the left in-ship-window's 'target' tab (standard-key: '1').

The manifest scanner is not only helpful if you are a pirate. It can also be useful to identify freight routes in the context of local policy.

The most important thing about the manifest scanner is that you are aware of the following fact:
As with the frame shift wake scanner , you might be mistaken for a pirate or even a ganker when in the vicinity of the Newbie systems, a community goal or engineer bases. Don't fly around with one of these installed when in open at these places.

6.3 Weapons

To get a closer look at weapons and their characteristics in Elite Dangerous, you first have to take a look at the damage model, i.e. the way damage occurs and is detected.

6.3.1 The Damage Model

Elite Dangerous's damage model distinguishes between different types of damage on several 'layers' and depending on a multitude of factors.

6.3.1.1. Raw Damage

The first 'path' of the damage model is 'raw' violence, and described as 'health' or 'raw damage value'. This damage refers to the occurrence of mechanical forces such as a collision or a ramming impact.

There are only two weapons that produce 'raw' damage: The rail gun and the plasma accelerator. Both deal about 80% of their damage as 'raw' damage to their target object. This peculiarity of these two weapons will be of greater importance in PvP later on, so please keep it in mind, even though this does not seem to relevant now.

6.3.1.2 Thermal Damage

The second 'path' of the damage model is 'thermal damage'.

The amount of thermal damage 'resistance' is displayed as a relative percentage at the right in-ship-window's 'ship' tab, sub tab 'statistics' (symbolized). A positive percentage shows more resistance toward thermal weapons than the base (raw) damage value. An absolute value can be created and displayed by exporting your current ship to coriolis.io – check the 'addons' chapter of this book for 'edmc', a tool that can help you do so.

Thermal damage is – surprise, surprise - generated by 'thermal' weapons such as lasers. The peculiarity is that shields that have not been improved by engineers have a slightly lower capability to withstand thermal damage from lasers ('thermal resistance') (approx. -20%) and a much higher damage capacity in regard to guns ('kinetic resistance') (approx. +40%) and missiles of all kind ('explosive resistance') (approx. +50%).

> **Notice:**
> Concentrate on using lasers for attacking shields and save on other weapons' ammo. Use all weapons at once when encountering very strong opponents ('full panic mode')

6.3.1.3 Kinetic Damage

The third 'path' of the damage model is 'kinetic' damage. Like thermal damage, it is depicted as a positive or negative resistance. Here it is important to know that the hull of the ship, as long as not improved by engineers - has a slightly lower resistance to kinetic weapons like cannons of all kind (about -20%) and explosive weapons like missiles of all kind (about -40%).

In order to use kinetic weapons effectively against enemies however, there is another important factor: size. Weapons have a "penetration factor" against hull that varies depending on the type and size of the weapon. If a weapon has a smaller penetration factor than its victim, there is a deduction in effectiveness when inflicting damage on hull. Therefore, regardless of the number of weapons per weapon type, the largest possible kinetic weapons are used. This advice may have exemptions, but in general you want to have a hard punch in the last phase of a fight.

A class 1 sized weapon will lose more than 50% of its damage capability when attacking a Federal Corvette or Imperial Cutter compared to attacking a small ship like an Eagle. A class 3 or class 4 sized weapon will only lose a small fragment of its 'punch' when attacking larger ships.

6.3.1.4. Explosive Damage

The fourth 'path' of the damage model is 'explosive' damage. This is also represented as resistance.

Since shields have a greatly increased (+50%) resistance to this kind of damage, but hull has a significantly weaker resistance (-40%), using missiles against shields (without modifications done by Horizon's engineers) is not a good idea.

Missiles of all kinds do a lot of damage to the hull of ships in all sizes. Use them wisely after shields have dropped.

6.3.1.5. Module Damage

The fifth path of the damage model is actually not one.

It describes a way of directly damaging installed modules on an enemy ship, which can lead to the module's intermittent or permanent failure. Partly with immobilizing consequences for the enemy's ship, partly with catastrophic consequences.

Module damage is dealt with separately later in this chapter, it does not require any special weapons, but can be increased by skillful weapon selection.

Apart from weapon damage on modules, heat damage should be mentioned. You should always keep an eye on your ship's temperature and avoid temperatures above 100% from which point on your installed modules will suffer from overheating damage. This can end fatally.

If you see your heat level approaching 100%, stop firing and stop boosting. In addition, check for the 'flame' symbol on your ship's (right of the radar) hologram. It depicts the usage of a weapon effect that increases heat on the ship that is fired at. Rare with NPC but quite often found on player ships which use Horizons' engineers.

6.3.2. Target Acquisition

There are three types of target acquisition on regular weapons.

6.3.2.1. Fixed Weapons

These weapons are rigidly mounted and do not capture a target, they only shoot straight ahead.

As always in Elite: One single sentence is not precise enough. A really rigid and non aiming weapon would be too much a pain, so someone in heaven (sic!) made fixed weapons target everything they see, like gimballed. Huge difference? They only see a few pixels around your aiming point.

In other words: Fixed weapons are fixed, but the are able to 'snap in' around a target. Target something, aim at it and you will see the aim gets some kind of 'lock' when near. It's minimal but helpful!

(If you think it's a ridiculous feature, do this: Unlock your target, then try to hit it with your fixed laser. You need much more precision.)

6.3.2.2 Gimballed Weapons

This weapon mount is able to target ships in the forward view of the ship, provided the target is "visible" to the weapon (check weapon placement!). Gimballed weapons do have a high target acquisition capacity - they hit a lot and precisely - but they're irritable by chaff (see 6.2.3.1. Chaff Launcher) and somewhat weaker than fixed weapons.

They are, in spite of everything, of utmost importance especially for the beginner, as they are not only comfortable (and hit more than a person without practice), but above all eliminate the dangerous target fixation: Instead of constantly annoying yourself as a beginner with "I'll still get you" followed by ramming yourself to death by running into your opponent, you simply always aim somewhere a bit below your opponent: the weapons pursue the target upwards, no ramming damage, all good.

6.3.2.3. Turreted Weapons

With this weapon mount, the target guidance not only tracks targets in the direct frontal field of view, but in all areas visible to the weapon. Depending on its placement, the radius can reach up to approximately 180 degrees. Turreted weapons are more likely to miss their target and they are usually not perfect in their target guidance. They are like gimballed weapons easily irritable by chaffing and altogether weaker than gimballed weapons.

6.3.3 Types of weapons

Now it's getting really exciting, because the choice of the right weapon can literally save your ship.

6.3.3.1 Thermal weapons

Thermal weapons are named for their damage to the 'thermal' path of the damage model. They do not heat up an enemy ship in combat.

Thermal weapons basically include all laser variants: Pulse, Burst and Beam Lasers. (The mining laser only roasts a few forgotten steaks on the enemy's ship hull, but even that's doubtful. Also the powerplay mining laser 'mning lance' provided to peasants of Zamina Torval produces some damage but it's fixed and not really efficient in combat).

All lasers have one characteristic in common: they start losing their abilitiy to inflict damage after a very short distance (pulse and burst lasers from 500m, the beam laser variant from 600m, which doesn't really make a difference).

As a result, at a distance of 1500m, these lasers are primarily a light show, but no longer causing much damage. They are even worse with small and agile ships, because with increasing distance they usually miss these targets anyway.

There is hardly any difference between the pulse laser and the burst laser. As a rule, the burst laser is slightly stronger (+10%) with a bit more energy consumption (+10%) drawn from the power distributor. In addition, the burst laser generates more heat (+50%), but this increase in heat is usually only noticed in larger ships, because although the temperature is increasing, pulse and burst lasers still generate relatively little heat compared to the beam laser.
So pulse lasers and burst lasers are only of small difference, because even the penetration force on hulls and the damage of modules by fallen shields is almost the same. In general, the burst laser is the better choice for beginners, as it produces a little more damage per time, with about the same endurance.

The one difference that is worth to think about is the way the single shots are produced. Using a fixed weapon, the pulse laser is usually the easier to keep on target. This comes down to personal preference in the end, though.

The beam laser has about 25-33% more damage capability than the other two lasers, but with enormous disadvantages: Not only is it a lot more expensive, it also requires around 5.5 - 6 times as much electricity from the power distributor. This means that you can fire a maximum of 1/6 of the duration of the other lasers. In addition, the beam laser generates a considerable heat load, which is almost twice as high as that of a pulse laser and still at least 25% higher than that of a burst laser. Even the slightly higher effect against hulls of larger ships does not make the beam laser any better.

The bottom line is that for beginners, the burst laser is the way to go. The disadvantages of the alway-empty-when-needed-most beam laser – its cruel power distributor surge disqualifies it for new commanders. If you then take a look at the crappy efficiency of the beam laser in terms of converting distributor energy into damage done it finally gets really bad:

Usually, fights are not done 'dogfight' style, but in attack waves. Especially so at earlier stages and against NPC.

You fire at the enemy while flying towards him, then you place yourself behind him in a safe place. There you recharge your systems and eventually your shields using a shield cell bank.
While firing at your enemy, you shoud use 4 "pips" in "SYS" branch of your power distributor to provide maximum shield strength. A typical setting for this is "4-2-0", i.e. "4 in SYS - 2 in ENG - 0 in WEP".

You can either use 4-1-1 (SYS/ENG/WEP) or 4-2-0 (SYS/ENG/WEP). Fire duration using 1 in WEP is not significantly increased over 0 in WEP, but keeping 1 in ENG might give you that little bit of additional manouevrability that is not only fun but quite helpful in dodging enemy fire.

Let's take another Cobra Mk 3, not improved by Horizon's engineers, as an example, and equip it first with 2 x gimballed class 2 beam lasers, then with 2 x gimballed class 2 burst lasers, both with the largest and best power distributor you can install: class 3A, and compare the damage done.

Burst laser:

2 x class 2 Power distributor 3A with 24 MJ capacity
2 x 10.3 MJ/s damage (= approx. 20.6 MJ/s)
2 x 0.49 MJ/s power draw from distributor
(= approx. 0.98 MJ/s)

This results in a fire duration using one completely filled power distributor 'bucket' of

24 MJ / 0.98 MJ/s = approx. 24 seconds.

This results in a total damage of:

20.6 MJ x 24 s = approx. 495 MJ
In comparison to this, now the

Beam laser:

2 x class 2 Power distributor 3A with 24 MJ capacity
2 x 12.52 MJ/s damage (= approx. 25 MJ/s)
2 x 3.44 (!) MJ/s power draw from distributor
(= approx. 6.88 MJ/s)

This results in a fire duration using one completely filled power distributor 'bucket' of 24 MJ / 6.88 MJ/s= approx. 3.5 seconds.

And thus a total damage of:
25 MJ x 3.5 s = approx. 87.5 MJ

In terms of efficiency of a single "WEP" charge, there is a damage inflicted on your enemy's ship of approx. 87.5 MJ with the beam laser and of approx. 495 MJ with the burst laser. This provides a factor of almost 5.5 times the damage caused by the burst laser over the beam laser due to its phenomenally low distributor draw.

If this were the only factor in equipping ships with weapons, then the elite universe would be something for 8-year-olds. However, many factors are to be taken into account in the choice of weapons. A fire duration of 24 seconds is far too much even with very agile and fast ships that enjoy a lot of "time on target". It makes more sense to choose weapons that - if no ammo is used as in guns - provide about 10-15 seconds of fire time, depending on what you plan to fight and how you plan your attack distances and attack waves. This not as a 'git gud' advice but to mention the enormous complexity of Elite's combat functions.

Tip:
Only use beam lasers (when not engineered for efficiency by Horizons' engineers) on large ships going after NPC enemies. Using beams on smaller or medium sized ships against players is a recipe for disaster.

General recommendation: Burst laser (or pulse laser)

Recommendation for large ships vs NPC: Beam lasers

> **Important:** As soon as engineers are possible with the Horizons package, all this is suddenly no longer valid. You can then create the wildest combinations of basic weapon, modification and special effect... there will soon be another book dealing specifically with the ideal combinations of engineers and other possibilities offered by the Horizons package.

6.3.3.2 Kinetic Weapons

Kinetic weapons fire projectiles in an ancient tradition and create 'kinetic' damage on an enemy's ship. Unlike lasers, kinetic weapons are not nearly as similar to each other, though.

The all-purpose weapon among the kinetic weapons is the multi-cannon. Similar to 19th-21st 'Gatling' machine guns, these weapons fire salvos of small projectiles with a high cadence (firing frequency) and quite high projectile speed.

For this reason, the multiple cannon is a good all-rounder in every respect: it has a very low energy consumption from the power distributor (resulting in a long fire duration), it has plenty of ammunition and its high projectile speed allows a large range and at the same time prevents the opponent from really successfully dodging the projectiles. In addition, the high projectile speed needs less 'lead' on a target, which makes keeping track much easier than with 'slow' weapons.

Multi-cannons are not very strong against modules, but they deliver a reliable and steady flow (interrupted by reloading) of damage toward your enemy.

Like all kinetic weapons, the multi-cannon is optimized for hull damage and weaker on shields than comparable lasers.

The multi-cannon can be fired at distances of up to 3 km, but using it usually makes most sense at a distance of below 2 km in distance, otherwise the hit rate will drop too much.

As an alternative, the classic cannon is quite popular with "commanders", but I would advise beginners against it.

The cannon has a much lower damage potential than the multiple cannon because its low projectile speed produces a high number of misses.

When the cannon hits, its damage is comparable to that of a multi-cannon, but this rarely happens without additional tuning by Horizons' engineers at distances of more than 1000 meters. If you want to fight with cannons, you should be able to fly excellently and 'dance' very close to your opponent with an agile ship. With cannons it's 'hug your enemy!'.

The cannon has a real right to exist, especially in large versions - as a powerful module killer. Once the shields are down and you have a direct line of sight to a vulnerable and combat-critical module like the power plant, a single shot from a class 4 cannon can put an end to that very module. With a severely damaged power plant, your enemy becomes a sitting duck.

The cannon is not a wise choice for beginners, especially when not engineered (Horizons!) for a higher projectile speed (long rande modification).

The third kinetic weapon is the fragment cannon.

The smallest gimballed fragment cannon class 1 does more than 36 MJ of kinetic damage with three consecutive shots (one salvo). In size (class) 3, it delivers up to 115 MJ in one salvo (fixed version). Engineered, up to 280 MJ. Fragment cannons are real killers.

Unfortunately, this 'killer' flag is not only valid in terms of damage to your enemy. 'Frags' can kill you, too:

The fragment cannon is a kind of suicide mission for beginners. This is because their range is enormously limited due to their spread. Even larger ships must be fired at on distances less than 600 (!) meters in order to fully use their potential. Fragment cannons have a wide spread / dispersion / cone of fire and additional 'falloff' weakening over a comparably short distance.

Smaller ships sometimes require even shorter distances to not waste too much of 'the cone'. All this under fire, because the opponent normally does not sleep but attack you.
In medium-sized and larger ships, especially with the help of the engineers, there are plenty of possibilities for using the fragment cannons or the even more improved 'pacifier' fragment cannon, which can be obtained by participating in power play, pledged to 'Zachary Hudson'. However, they are also legendary 'assault weapons', which doesn't necessarily make you the most loved person in game. Simply having them installed makes you a suspect for being an assassin or even a ganker.

In general one should consider the following things when selecting kinetic weapons:

Kinetic weapons need a 'lead' angle. Due to its comparatively low projectile speed (worst of all: the cannon), one (or the gimballed/turret mount) has to aim at the point where the sent projectile will hopefully meet the enemy's ship after travelling some distance. The greater this distance, the longer the journey, the higher the possibility that an abrupt change of the enemy's direction will result in a missed shot.

If you get involved in a cornering battle or fight a faster ship, it will usually move upwards in your own field of vision as you instinctively position it that way – it's only human.

If you have mounted kinetic weapons on the underside of your ship, their "field of view" is more limited the further back they are mounted, creating a huge 'dead spot' above a certain position in your forward view.

With a Cobra Mk3, for example, this means that a cannon has the greatest difficulty in reaching a target even halfway up the field of view, since the angle of attack is considerably higher and the cannon cannot aim at targets in this area (it would hit its own ship).

So it makes sense to mount a kinetic weapon on the top or the side of the ship as it is the only way for the weapon to maintain its 'lead' angle properly.

Another important thing with kinetic weapons is their main purpose: damaging the hull. As already mentioned above, weapons are equipped with a so-called "penetration factor". The same applies to hulls. If the penetration factor of a weapon is smaller than that of the hull, it receives a deduction from the assessed damage. (There is no bonus the other way around).

Since kinetic weapons almost always require less energy than their colleagues from the 'thermal' side aka lasers, the decision (as a basic rule) is simple:

> **Tip:**
> The large weapon hardpoints are used for kinetic weapons (if they are on the upperside or if they are at least far forward when below).

6.3.3.3 Explosive Weapons

The third category of weapons covers everything that explodes in some way.

The simplest variant of it are mines. These unguided bombs are simply "dropped" in the hope that a ship will get into their vicinity, triggering them to explosion.

Mines exist as regular mines and as shock mines. The latter are a few percent less strong in damage done but shake their victim 'like a polaroid picture'. Seriously, shock mines provide enough rapid displacement for making it very hard to hit you, especially when using fixed weapons.

The problem with mines is that more proficient 'commanders' as most higher ranked NPC won't be surprised by them and evading them is quite easy.

Mines are – for exactly this reason – a clear 'not recommended', especially for new commanders. They can be a real threat, though: After Horizons' engineers' treatment, they can utilize an effect that can kill shield generators. Not by emptying your shield damage capacity but by killing your shield generator through your shields. Be careful when attacked by humans with mines (same with torpedoes).

A little more effort is required with dumbfire missiles. These weapons, which are not equipped with a targetting function, are sent in the right direction manually and do about 50MJ of explosive damage per shot. That sounds tempting at first. Until you learn how hard it is to hit something with their comparably slow 'projectile' speeds. These missiles can be dodged quite easily and the sustained damage over time is very low due to the high miss rate, the low cadence and the long reload times. In the end you can add a hefty bonus on your ammo restock bills and sob silently.

Dumbfire missiles are not recommended for beginners, but they do fit a certain purpose when you're more experienced. Be it for the extra punch when your opponent's shields have dropped or for a special effect by Horizon's engineers that can disrupt a Frame Shift Drive – which makes running away from ships equipped with these a quite hard task.

Seeker missiles are the next evolutionary step. Their aiming apparatus needs some time to 'find a lock' , but when 'locked' and fired, they pursue their target with great tenacity over longer distances and at comparatively high speed – and still deliver about 40 MJ of explosive damage.

However, seeker missiles are quickly eliminated by point defenses (see 6.2.3.6. Point Defense) and therefore ineffective when encountering ships using these. And as if that were not enough, electronic countermeasures (see point 6.2.3.2. EGM) can quickly put them into sleep mode. Although they will finally wake up from that nap after some time, but their target must be in their vicinity to reactivate their hunt.

This failure rate and their high cost make them prohibitive for new commanders.

Torpedoes are a special case, but not a very good one.

These "huge missiles" do much more damage than missiles (about 120 MJ of explosive damage), but they are extremely slow (about 250 m/s) and one can easily evade them. Torpedoes should only be fired at a distance of 1-2 km, while the opponent comes into your direction, ideally in a straight line. Even with the best timing, some torpedoes miss their target - and that at horrendous cost.

Torpedoes are a NO GO for beginners and an unwise choice later on if not modded by Horizon's engineers.

6.3.3.4. Weird Weapons

Naming of this category is not to be understood as derogatory, it's more a smiling acknowledgement of Elite's diversity.

The 'weirdest' weapon first:
The rail gun. This weapon is only available (so far) in classes 1 and 2 and this for a good reason: Its heat development and energy requirements from the power distributor are huge. They are therefore used, when not improved by Horizon's engineers (to reduce heat and increase efficiency), as weapons-of-opportunity.

A rail gun must be manually aimed at the target and has no gimballed or turreted version available. In addition, it must be charged for three seconds before firing. In other words, you hold down the fire button for three (long) seconds while tracking your target and keeping it in aim... for three (long) seconds. Then and only then will you be rewarded with up to 40 MJ of Class 2 rail cannon damage.

Then why bother?

Not at all as a beginner!

Later on you will like a little specialty about the rail gun: The rail cannon has an advantage in delivering 80% of its damage to the 'raw damage' path, i.e. the 40 MJ damage is not delivered to one of the resistances such as 'thermal' or 'kinetic', but to the base value of the shields. This advantage is not an advantage for beginners, because at this stage the fewest 'commanders' operate shields with low base values and high resistances and computer opponents even less so.

Rail guns are only mentioned for beginners because they are 'something special' or in cause you want to practice for your glorious future PvP career.

The second 'weird' weapon is the plasma accelerator.

This weapon is available in class 2-4 and it's quite similar to a regular cannon. It fires plasma projectiles that travel at a slow speed and can easily be dodged. If they hit, they do a lot of damage: A simple 'class 2 plasma accelerator' inflicts 55 MJ of damage, 80% of this in 'raw' damage.

Unfortunately, the plasma accelerator is also extremely energy-hungry and therefore not only will WEP always be empty when you are about to fire, but also the damage value over a longer period of time suffers from it. It's a so called 'alpha damage' weapon that inflicts high damage on its first shot, then a radically slower rate of damage due to energy consumption.

In addition there is a high miss rate, because the low projectile speed makes hits over 1000m of distance a rare occasion. All in all, the plasma accelerator, like the rail gun, is not a weapon for beginners, unless you want to work consistently towards a PvP career later on by practicing early.

Also in the 'weird weapons' category there is another weapon that is not so weird at all after a short explanation: It is powerful, it does immense damage, it has plenty of ammunition and it is not too difficult to hit something with it: YOUR SHIP.

> **Pro-Tip:**
> **Ramming is a weapon of its own, inflicting massive damage onto your enemy. And yourself.**

The question of 'who's going to hurt whom more?' in ramming is not easy to decide by ship size. Rather, the movement of both ships generates kinetic energy (physics, not the 'kinetic' damage path. Damage done is 'raw'), which is then distributed to the "accident partners". Keywords physics teaching, inelastic impact, energy conservation theorem.....

If you have intact shields on your ship and your opponent is 'shields down', there is nothing wrong with a juicy ram shot using '4 in SYS' versus ships of about the same size. If you both got weak shields or if you both are 'shields down', you should only perform a ram if you know about the stability of your ship (and that of the opposing ship), knowing you're stronger.

It is important to know that your own speed as well as the impact angle and the shape of the ships involved - Elite Dangerous is really taking all that into account! - increases the damage done by a "grazing" wedge shaped Python, for example, significantly less than a "winged" Imperial Clipper that doesn't slide off.

With the Clipper, we're right on top of the subject: ramming computer opponents! Oh, yeah! On some NPC ships like the Clipper, ramming is one of the most dangerous features - and the beast sprints like a cat with someone steppign on its tail (please DO NOT try at home, cats are mostly very likeable creatures and deserve better. And you deserve better than a p***** off cat!). Let's just say the Clipper has some built in catapult and devastating ram capabilities.

So besides your own consideration of using your ship's hull as a weapon, always pay attention to your opponent. A 1000 ton clipper that spurts towards you at 450 m/s or more all at once, filling your windscreen, quickly makes the 250 tons of a Cobra Mk3 not only look old but also broken.

6.3.4 Module Damage

As described at the beginning of this chapter describing the damage model, modules can be damaged after shields dropped or in case shield generators are used in too small a size from the start.

To inflict module damage to your opponent, first use the 'Cycle modules' function (default key: "Z"). You will then receive information about all installed modules of the opponent, one after the other, as long as you have him as an active target.

If you do not want to cycle through the modules one by one, open the left ship-in window (standard key: "1") and switch to the 'target' tab. There you will find all his installed modules with percentages of system integrity.

If you now select a module (either by 'clicking' in the 'target' field or by manually cycling the modules), a "hitbox" appears on the target, a small red field in standard colors. If you hit a ship with dropped (or too small) shields into this field, the module beneath the surface takes damage.

Depending on the weapon used, the damage caused varies considerably and some weapons are known as real "module killers", such as large cannons or large plasma accelerators. If no module protection is installed and you have a free field of fire on the "coveted" module, for example the power plant, 1-2 shots can be sufficient with these weapons to paralyze the opponent.

On the defensive side, you should make sure that the modules that are important for a possible later escape are not 'exposed' to enemy fire: When shields drop, make sure you don't get hit into your thrusters (your back), your power plant and frame shift drive (check where these are on your ship type by targetting your ship type on some NPC or player) should not be presented to the opponent.

So here's the urgent advice: Boosting away while you're preparing to escape is often the worst option, especially if you still have some hull left. Turning towards the opponent while the jump drive is charging can have dramatic looking consequences like failing weapons, a destroyed canopy (with you going on helmet & oxygen), but what saves your life (the thrusters, your power plant and your FSD) remains untouched, because it is not in the line of fire. That's how you might get away with a black eye.

6.3.5 Engineers

First of all: If your ship is not improved by Horizon's engineers in terms of additional performance according to the current 'fight and combat ideal', please don't get involved in fights with other 'commanders', unless you have agreed to a training fight to 'shields down' or '50% hull' or whatever non lethal option both of you prefer. 'Fight to death' against human players in engineered ships without being 'up to the task' in performance is suicide!

The explanation for this rude judgement and this urgent advice is simple, let me give you an example: You got a ship with 100% offensive damage capability and 100% defensive stamina, so does your opponent with one little difference: He spent a few days using engineers. Now his ship adds 50% of offensive capabilities with modified weapons and another 50% because of a better power distributor. It has got at least 200% of your offensive power. Add special effects which can kill your shields in an instant or your shield cell banks. Add effects that can make you go blind on your target, make you go slower, make you tumble like mad. And this was only the offensive part...

The engineers are 'characters' (actually rather ship bases) to which you get access under a variety of conditions. Sometimes you have to travel 5000 light years for an engineer to give you access, sometimes you have to deliver tons of special cigars (no joke!). Even the mere acquaintance with an engineer can be linked to labour-intensive conditions.

If you reached 'access' level with the respective engineer, you bring him material(s) for the creation of an improvement: 'raw' material, to be found on planet surfaces, 'manufactured' material, to be found at conflict zones, resource zones, several different signal sources etc. and 'data', which is most often obtained by targetting random ships.

(This is a very vague description of material gathering. An in depth explanation will be found in the upcoming 'horizons and guardians' part of this book series).

Some of these materials can also - at unfavourable rates - be exchanged for each other at material dealers. These are to be found at some high tech systems (data), industrial systems (manufactured) and extraction/refinery systems (raw). Use inara.cz's 'nearest' finder to see a list of material traders close to you.

With full access, you order a 'modification' from the engineer of your choice: The first time you use an engineer on a certain weapon, you only got changes "grade 1" available, then also grade 2 to 5, depending on availability at the engineer and your 'standing' with the engineer: if you have had grade 1 created once, you get access to grade 2. If you have had it created at least 2x (sometimes even 3x – to the fullest), then you get access to grade 3. If you have had this grade created also 3 x (sometimes also 4x)... and so on.

Once you have unlocked grade 3 with the respective engineer, you can have an additional (special) effect applied for all modifications from grade 1.

It's important to always call the base improvements (the ones using grades) 'modifications' as too many commanders use sloppy terms for this. In addition, the term 'effect' is only used for additional effects on a weapon after a certain modification was done. It's a complex 'world', so get the other book ;-)

Want an example? I'd love to:

As a fan of old SOL-action-movies, you have installed a 'full Arnold' weapon setup on your Cobra Mk3: Four gimball-mounted multi-cannons. These are quite cool in regards to heat development and empty a full ammo clip or more per attack wave (see WEP capacity), but they're not the strongest and certainly not versus shields.

So you ask the engineer with the beautiful name Todd "The Blaster" McQuinn for a little more emphasis and have a modification called 'overcharged' applied to all the gimballed multi-cannons guns. One of the multi-cannons gets an additional special effect called 'corrosive' so that this gun softens the hull of the target after the shields have been lowered. Corrosive effects increases the damage done to hull by all weapons used because its effect is on the ship's hull, not on the weapon. Since kinetic weapons only produce kinetic damage, you have the three remaining weapons improved to 'incendiary' effect which converts some of the damage done to 'thermal' as if the guns were part laser.

Before the modifications, the offensive side of your Cobra looked like this:

With 4 pips in SYS for maximum shield strength, 0 in ENG for propulsion and 2 in WEP your cobra had about 26 seconds fire duration with about 10.8 MJ per second damage against shields and about 30 MJ per second damage against hull.

All in all, you could theoretically do ca. 285 MJ shield damage or about 780 MJ hull damage with one 'bucket' full of WEP energy.

After Todd has finished tinkering, your small power distributor only manages 16 seconds at a time, but with about 31 MJ per second against shields and about 60 MJ against hull (40.5 MJ/s plus "corrosive" effect that causes at least 50% more damage).

In the end, this results in approx. 480 MJ shield damage per WEP filling or approx. 960 MJ hull damage.

The little tinkering produces at least 50% more damage against shields and at least 20% more hull damage - carefully calculated.

In order to survive the battle against your Cobra Mk3 - tuned only in terms of weapons so far - another Cobra would have to have at least 50% more shield strength and at least 20% more hull strength. Impossible without engineers.

But that's not all. Engineers have a lot of additional 'cards up the sleeve': They can modify weapons which kill shield generators, inactivate shield cells when used, reboot frame shift drives, massively increase the heat level on your ship etc. etc. etc.

And those are just the guns. In addition, there are larger jumps, stronger shields, more powerful power stations, etc.

If you consider equipping and (fine-) tuning ships even a bit of fun, please consider purchasing the 'Horizons' package (and eventually the book about it being released soon). It is definitely worth it, because besides the engineers there are planetary landings, Guardians, Thargoids, Multicrew and many other things in it. In some way the basic package is the extended demo, the real fun is in the Horizons package.

6.3.6 When It Gets Dangerous.

There are four things you should always think about in combat. All of them have already been discussed in here before, but their importance makes me repeat them all once more:

4-in-SYS - Should be the basic rule in combat. If you can't think of anything useful to do while in combat, 4-in-SYS is vital. Using mouse and keyboard? Down arrow, left arrow twice. This results in about 250% shield strength compared to 0-in-SYS and is really decisive in every respect.

Shield Generators - These should always be large enough to cover the actual ship mass. If a shield generator is too small, i.e. its maximum mass does not cover the ship's mass, damage can occur to the hull and modules - with shields still intact! So please always check shield generator 'mass' and optimal shield mass, either in the outfitting area or by using coriolis.io

Ramming - Is a mess, but a valid part of fighting. Please be careful, though: it can also go really wrong. Always make sure you're on the winning side: more shields, more hull, more mass! And remember: Your opponent might have the same idea...

Dodge - It's not a pointless act, it's a valid part of fighting. Especially slow-flying weapons like plasma accelerators and larger cannons lose their might if you dodge and 'dance' continuously. This won't prevent all hits, but it reduces the overall damage enormously.

To do this, simply press and hold down the vector thrust (default key: "F") when flying up against the opponent. Then roll 10-20 degrees to the left or right every 10-20 seconds. Rolling too much or rolling too often reduces your 'dancing' as your vector movement must have a bit of time to build up. Too hectic manouevring makes you more predictable, as illogical as this might seem.

6.3.7 Miscellaneous

Should something not work properly after a more or less difficult fight – no Frame Shift Drive, no possibility to contact the station or similar, please open the right window in the ship (standard key: "4") and use the ship screen to search for "Reboot/Repair". Once selected, a 3-second countdown starts first, then the reboot sequence begins, where all modules are repaired makeshift. That doesn't mean that a 0% module gets 100% again, but usually it is to be brought back to life at least for a short time.

In the approximately 45 seconds of this function you are completely helpless and defenseless, so you should only use it if you are at least halfway safe. If the modules are not "healed" enough at the first restart, you can repeat the process 1-2 times.

7. External Information

Elite Dangerous had a difficult birth. After the 1993 version of Elite was so hopelessly unstable and bug ridden that it was almost unbearable for non occasional players, the 1995 version that followed as a solution (yes, things were slower in pre-internet times) could not really make up for the damage done.

David Braben, the head of Frontier Developments, had promised again and again in the then following 15+ years to bring a new Elite version to life, but this has failed for various reasons, one of which is probably the lack of capital for a project of this size in a dire phase of the gaming industry. 'Did you hear? A new Elite version is in the talks again!' was some kind of a running gag.

In 2013, Braben's company Frontier Development announced a low budget approach: A crowdfunding project to revive a basic version of Elite Dangerous with an ongoing development being financed on its sales. A release for the end of 2014 was planned. This low budget approach created a huge group of 'backers' funding the project and 'beta testing' Elite Dangerous. It also created dozens of 'community' projects in regard to wikis, databases and tools.
Elite's 'Player Base' is loyal, active and highly competent.

This chapter shows you some of the most important websites about Elite Dangerous. Of course there are countless others, but most of them are redundant or variations of the ones presented here. With these, most of what you need is covered – for now.

7.1 Finding things

Elite is a complex thing and you often need to find things somewhere:

- systems
- stages
- ships
- modules
- Materials for Intenieurs
- trade routes

And more. A lot more. Instead of using the galaxy map and going places or combing through countless reddit or forum postings, just use this website:

www.EDDB.IO
(www.eddb.io)

Eddb receives live in game data from commanders, maintaining a giant database of all ingame data available.

Depending on the type of data, most of it is highly up-to-date (the "ticker" of the background simulator, which runs every afternoon, and the "correction ticker" in the morning make certain things like the current state of the system sometimes a little uncertain in economic terms, but before you start longer journeys based on eddb data, you can validate the data briefly on the galaxy and system maps. In general you should use data marked as being 'younger' over older data.)

If you want to help keep eddb.io's data up to date (and other community projects based on it) automatically every time you dock, please read below about the little tool called 'Elite Dangerous Market Connector' – it will not only update eddb.io but help you out on a few other things.

Example about eddb.io?

You are looking for a place near your current system "Ehecatl" that sells an ASP Explorer. You need good thrusters (5A), a good frame shift drive (5A) and good shields (6A) together with some shield boosters (0A).

You open eddb.io and use the station finder.

Under 'ship' you choose the ASP Explorer, under 'modules' you choose the modules mentioned above. After a click on 'search' a list appears.

You can sort this list, normally you choose 'lowest distance' for convenience.

Now you can simply click on the corresponding station to learn more about it - or simply copy & paste it into the galactic map in game to create a route there.

Without eddb.io, searching for ships and modules, especially the larger ones, is a real pain, depending on your location and how much knowledge you got about the systems around you.

Please be aware: eddb.io exists because of countless 'man hours' invested. If you like it, please consider searching for its 'donate' button by scrolling down. It's small, they're humble people...

7.2 Building Ships

Shipbuilding is a very complex business, often accompanied by some real effort in making modules work together in a useful way while keeping energy requirements 'in check'.

Apart from having a general idea of what your future ship shall be able to do for you, it's extremely important to see the build you're planning to create really delivers.

Two websites have collected all data of all components with great effort and turned them into real Elite Dangerous ship configurators with impressive programming effort:

CORIOLIS.IO
(coriolis.io)

and

EDSHIPYARD.COM
(edshipyard.com)

At the time of printing edshipyard.com is under construction - please check its beta button before you decide which configurator you want to use. Edshipyard was ahead for a long time, but Coriolis has become more and more the reference as it uses an emphasis on relevant data shown.

Two important tips about Coriolis.io:

1. Coriolis can create short links to your ship (chain symbol in the top right corner), this is very helpful if you want to send it to someone experienced for a second opinion).

2. You can export your current ship (in game) to the coriolis.io configurator using the already mentioned 'Elite Dangerous Market Connector', which is described below. This function is extremely helpful and convenient if you want to 'fiddle around' with different options before improving a current ship.
Please don't be discouraged at first. Both, coriolis and edshipyard can shock you with their vast amount of (partly cryptic) information and their abundance of options. Play around, it's free and it will help you a lot in understanding ships in Elite Dangerous.

Edshipyard and coriolis.io are free to use. Please be aware that creating this kind of web project is a labor intensive thing. Be so nice to consider donating to them if you use one of them. Edshipyard's donate button is to be found in the top right corner (at least in 'modern' view), coriolis' donate button is hidden behind 'settings' followed by 'about'.

7.3 News, Information and Space Selfies

Since one of Elite Dangerous' main features is being a 'construction' game, a world in which you live, perform, grow and prosper, it's only natural that you want to show it.

A wonderful website - actually THE ONE website par excellence is

INARA.CZ
(inara.cz)

This english-language website not only provides the option of creating a personal profile of you and your activities so that the whole world can see what a 'great' commander you are, inara.cz is also a discussion platform and information source similar to eddb.io.

It's definitely worth registering there (it's free). Not only is inara.cz the first port of call when 'background checking' whether the commander you just met is 'a white hat' or a 'bad guy', inara.cz can also be enormously helpful:

Coupling inara.cz with the above mentioned "Elite Dangerous Market Connector" results in a unique combination: Elite Dangerous always reports the current state of stored materials for engineers to inara.cz. With the help of custom 'cooking recipes' in your personal 'crafting list', you can always keep an eye on what is still missing for the next ship project. This avoids ineffective material gathering and gives you comfort of thought when finally travelling to distant engineers.

As with the other mentioned community tools, I can only ask you politely to donate to them in case you use it on a more regular basis. Inara.cz has an enormous depth and Artie (its founder) is really tireless in upgrading the website and its functions. You can find the extremely small 'donation' link in the footer of each page.

7.4 Addons

These little helpers can make life easier for you in game.

Perhaps the most important tool (which has already been mentioned) is the

Elite Dangerous Market Connector (EDMC)

This small Windows program can be downloaded from github (a large developer platform) - the easiest way is to simply copy its name (see above) into the search engine of your choice. The installation is short and self-explanatory, the program is supplied with your Frontier access data the first time it is started and it's ready to go.

The Elite Dangerous Market Connector (short: edmc) appears as a normal program with the data of the commander, the ship name and the system name. If you are docked at a station it's also shown.

If you click on the ship name, the magic starts: Your current ship is exported to one of the ship configurators described above (which one depends on your selection in edmc's options) and can be used to 'play through possible improvements 'in dry dock'. This function is worth its weight in gold.

If you click on the system or station name, you will see information depending on which 'display target' you have selected in the options before.

And 'edmc' can do even more for you: If you are registered at inara.cz, you can get the API key in its personal area and save it in edmc's options. From this point on, any changes to the cargo (including engineering materials) and the ship, as well as any missions carried out, launches, etc., are automatically taken from the Elite Dangerous journal and transfered directly into inara.cz. This not only eliminates the annoying manual entries in inara.cz to keep your data up to date, but also provides additional information that you would not otherwise have had available.

If you can live with the fact that a small tool from github handles your Frontier login data data (there hasn't been a single security incident with edmc in all those years that I know of and if you use an Android smartphone...), you have a wonderful tool with edmc that makes your work a lot easier.

As with the websites available, I wish to mention that creating such a tool and maintaining it is hard work and very time consuming. If EDMC is of any help for you – and I bet it is – please consider donating to the project:

https://paypal.me/Xant

Elite Dangerous Recon (EDR)

EDR was originally born out of the desire to pursue 'bad boys' - it should automatically transfer sightings of questionable figures to bounty hunters.

Unfortunately, despite the clear need, EDR has reached too few 'customers' to be able to reliably hunt bounties - although the information provided is helpful and numerous.

Commander Lekeno did not give up and extended EDR successively by further functions. It is now - after registration - not only able to maintain a kind of "personal contact file", it also possesses rich information about obtaining sought-after engineering materials and tools to fly to their sources professionally and error-free.

EDRecon ist downloadable here:

https://edrecon.com/

Please consider donating to CMDR Lekeno's EDR project if it improves your space life. He doesn't really point at it, so this is his patreon link:

https://www.patreon.com/lekeno

8. Connect To People

Elite Dangerous isn't a classic MMO, but it has a huge potential (maybe because of that) to find new "in game" friends.

Please be aware that Elite Dangerous pairs 'commanders' according to 'IP geolocation', according to ship type and equipment, according to behavior and many other factors. There are usually only a few 'commanders' in an 'instance', i.e. within a part of the world visible to them – there might be many more you won't see, right next to you. There are systems with 3000 or more ships a day, most of them being residents, and you normally 'see' only 5-10 of these, especially when you're one of the more 'steady' commanders: Same ship, same weapons, same activity all the time.

If you want to meet with friends, they should at least be in your friends list. The matchmaker will always try to bring friends into a common shared instance. By the way, this also has an effect on the whole game experience: If you have 'bad' friends, you are more likely to encounter other 'bad guys' - at least if the 'bad' friends are currently online.

If meeting your friend(s) does not work, just create a temporary 'wing' in game. This wing then more or less forces all wing members into one instance - which usually works. If not: Simply jump into another system and then back. This reinitiates your instancing.

8.1 Making Friends

Before you have friends in your friends list, you have to get to know them first.

Real "people" around you can be identified on the radar screen as unfilled (hollow) symbols. If you have such a symbol on your screen, you can either point at it with your ship's nose (and use it as target) to find out the name of the "commander", or you can start a "round call" into local chat.

With the name of the commander you can click on the "man with shadow" symbol above chat menu (default key: "E"). If there is no cursor, and then address him - and only him - with a direct (private) message.

If you don't have a name of a specific commander or if you just want to say 'hello' to the people around you, just press the return key and you can write into 'local' chat (no name visible). Should a name appear by mistake, please write '/l' (small 'L') without quotation marks to address the local chat (everything in the area).

If you don't see any other contacts, but assume that there are more people in the system, you can also use the system chat. Just write '/s' or '/system' at the beginning of the line (again without quotation marks). However, this function is still somewhat unreliable.

> Important: The system chat is normally not visible. If the chat is opened you can toggle between the regular chat view and the system view using 's' and 'w' for 'down' and 'up'.

If you think that you have never had a "commander" on your screen before, then look at the "clock" symbol above: There you can see who is near you at the moment ("now") and who it was (with time).

8.2 The Squadrons

If you are a group person, you might want to join a group of players who have similar interests.

In game there is also the Squadrons function, accessible via the right status window (standard key "4").

The problem here is that the description of squadrons is quite poor and many have not enabled the 'quick join' feature.

Either way, before joining a group, you should take your time to find out what the group really is like and not just read its marketing leaflet.

Example: In the former main starter system (now 'for experienced players') Eravate, you'll sometimes encounter a notorious group of players, pretending to be 'protectors of newbie space'. They tell fabulous tales of being a helpful group, defending newbies, helping out and more. In reality, the group has mostly helped new commanders only for recruitment or for improving public relations and their 'defense' has attracted more socially awkward and aggressive people to Eravate than anything or anyone else. In addition they quite often act aggressively and in a questionable way (keeping a 'kill on sight' list, bullying people in wings of 4, all justified by their 'protector' role).

Think twice before joining such a group, ask around and use a search engine to get a picture of it in advance.

> Pro-Tip: When talking to members of a group you wish to join, you can often see their 'alignment' by checking their language. 'L33T 5P34K' for example is more for the younger, more active, more 'gaming' oriented commander, to say it nicely.

Other groups might be small and hard to find because they're not recruiting by force (seriously, there's a group at Eravate telling people 'join or die', destroying your ship if you don't join them...) or recruiting en masse to become as large as possible in the shortest time span. These often are the real gems.

You can find all kinds of groups in terms of orientation and size on inara.cz's squadron pages. Go there, have a look. Elite is more fun when with some non-intrusive buddies.

At this point I would like to point out again that the 'minor factions' in Elite are often player factions. For example, you support cmdr pink velvet's (random name) kindergarten group by simply docking at Cleve Hub or Ackerman Station in Eravate and doing business there. Or by doing missions for their small faction in one of their other mostly deserted systems. Every activity that creates income on your side at their stations benefits them, so do missions for their minor factions. Easy as that. If you don't want to support a certain player group's minor faction go elsewhere or solely do missions for other minor factions in their system.

Remember, in Elite, the little man 'on the street' has power. His actions strengthen or weaken these (player) factions immensely.

You have power!

8.3 Discord

There are countless chat servers on Discord about Elite Dangerous, but most of them are either for powerplay groups (Zachary Hudson, Aisling Duval etc.) or maintained by Squadrons.

An open discord, which was created together with the biggest reddit group, is the EDRD Discord.

The invitation link to this discord is:

https://discord.gg/elite

If you decide to visit this discord, please remember that it is one of the more civilized places in the "gaming world" and people there help with great willingness. The tone is usually accordingly friendly and polite. If you ever encounter "black sheep", please do not hesitate to inform the moderators about them.

9. Hardware: Keyboard, Mouse, HOTAS...

One of the most common questions beginners ask is how to choose the right input device and then the right product.

In general: Choose the input method that suits you. If you like to fly with a joystick or HOTAS, use that. If you enjoy mouse and keyboard, it's okay. If you're more of a console fan, use a controller. But please keep reading anyway.

The combination of mouse and keyboard is certainly not the one that lets you immerse yourself in the world of elite - keyword "immersion".

However, in addition to the lower cost factor, the mouse and keyboard have another major advantage over other input options: precision.

A large part of those who like to do combat in Elite are using mouse and keyboard. The mouse has the greatest precision for the use of (non-targeted) weapons and the keyboard, which seems confusing at first, is simply enormously versatile when it comes to special configurations.

A special keyboard is not necessary, the same applies to the mouse. For both, however, it is helpful to use models with integrated macro functions, as these allow switching between power distribution settings and other functions within seconds.

By the way: The use of macro-enabled input devices is not a 'disgraceful topic' in Elite - it is even recommended in the general consensus of the players! (Although some self proclaimed heroes... shrug them off.)

If you don't want to change your keyboard or if you have a limited budget, you prefer a macro mouse to a macro keyboard. In addition to a fine resolution of the mouse, the presence of at least 3 easily accessible (thumb?!) macro keys is particularly advantageous.

In the following you will find some examples and buying tips. To make it easier for you to find the product you are looking for, there is always the QR-Code to scan underneath, you will then be lead directly at the corresponding product on Amazon.

For the sake of simplicity I have put together the above collected links to the best input devices for you and put them on my website for you to click on:

https://www.ed-howto.com/suggenstions

10. Outlook

As already mentioned extensively in the preface, this book is not a complete work. That is simply not possible in this size, since the elite world is not only ancient, but above all huge.

For this reason there will - hopefully soon - be additional books dealing with the advanced topics individually. Among other things about engineers, advanced combat and individual ship types.

You can also find more information and announcements as well as news regarding updates and news at

https://www.ed-howto.com

So, have fun playing, always a good flight and "Stay tuned".

11. Annex: Road To Riches – The List

Nr	Systemname	Objekt(e)	Distanz
1	Trappist-1	4	42,4
2	HIP 114458	A 2	103,7
3	HIP 116600	6	71,0
4	HIP 5845	A3	92,3
5	HIP 10047	12	60,0
6	HIP 10972	AB 1	26,6
7	Arietis Sector FL-Y c7	A 1	62,8
8	HIP 19217	7	36,2
9	Hyades Sector GB-X c1-21	1	40,6
10	HIP 21078	A7	42,7
	-> Ab hier: Pfadfinder Rang, 10 Millionen credits		
11	Col 285 Sector DV-Y d53	2 + 3	43,2
12	Col 285 Sector IL-X c1-12	1	14,8
13	HIP 22105	6	25,7
14	HIP 21863	A6	27,2
15	HIP 22306	4	23,8
16	HIP 19637	A 4 + A 5	52,0
17	Pleiades Sector KH-V c2-13	10	49,8
18	Pleiades Sector IR-W d1-36	5 a	31,8
19	HIP 17873	4	45,4
20	Synuefe ME-O b39-0	A2	77,4
21	Synuefe ER-V c18-5	2	48,8
22	HIP 15977	B 4	45,8
23	Synuefe JS-T c19-2	6	70,5
24	HIP 10697	10	50,0
25	HIP 10796	A4 + 2 weitere	75,6
26	Aries Dark Region HR-W d1-63	3	71,0
27	HIP 11316	2	59,2
28	Aries Dark Region GW-W c1-0	1	53,8
29	Mel 22 Sector NI-T d3-16	A 5	35,7
30	Mel 22 Sector PA-D b13-0	A 5	69,4
31	Mel 22 Sector NI-T d3-18	8	10,4
32	Mel 22 Sector JC-V d2-46	A 3	35,7
33	Mel 22 Sector WA-M b8-2	6	76,5
34	Taurus Dark Region HR-W c1-7	6	37,1
35	Taurus Dark Region QT-R b4-0	A 3	42,8

Nr	Systemname	Objekt(e)	Distanz
36	Mel 22 Sector FR-V c2-3	3	64,3
37	HIP 18119	6	36,4
38	Hind Sector AQ-Y d12	AB 1	66,6
39	Hind Sector LN-T c3-2	2	36,1
40	Hind Sector RT-R c4-5	A 1	75,2
41	Hind Sector KX-T c3-0	A 12	60,6
42	Taurus Dark Region FL-Y d19	7	54,5
43	HIP 23949	9	36,8
44	Mel 22 Sector JM-K b9-0	6	76,9
45	Synuefe VZ-E b31-3	5	51,5
46	Synuefe PI-B c16-4	A 2	65,8
47	Mel 22 Sector WZ-E b12-2	7	33,7
48	Mel 22 Sector UO-Q c5-4	A 6	44,2
49	Synuefe MP-M d8-56	6	111,5
50	Synuefe IJ-O d7-47	C 3	57,8
51	Synuefe MP-M d8-18	A 2	45,8
52	Synuefe NP-M d8-52	11	31,9
53	Synuefe WO-Z c16-9	3	80,4
54	Synuefe UT-Z c16-14	1	40,7
55	Synuefe UT-Z c16-17	2	26,5
56	Synuefe GT-O d7-79	5	110,5
57	Synuefe KZ-M d8-77	2	59,6
58	Wregoe KX-L d7-77	5	104,5
59	Wregoe LI-K d8-63	4	147,5
60	Wregoe LI-K d8-20	4	69,7

Printed in Great Britain
by Amazon